Julius Caesar: Siege of Marseille

Christopher Gunstone

BA Hons History and Archaeology, ACIM.

Copyright © 2022 by Christopher Gunstone
Published by Silver Shields
www.silvershields.co.uk

All rights reserved. This book or any portion thereof may not be reproduced or used in any manner whatsoever without the express permission of the publisher except for the use of brief quotations embodied in critical reviews and certain other non-commercial uses permitted by copyright law.

Printed by KDP.

C. Gunstone, *Julius Caesar: Siege of Marseille,* Silver Shields, 2022

Subjects:
History > Ancient > General
History / General
History / Greece / Rome / France
Social Science / Archaeology

Includes, Endnotes, References, Index,
110 pages and 19 Illustrations.

ISBN: 979-8408681754

DEDICATION

☙ ❧

To my Mother and Father for their encouragement and support.

The Ancient Greeks whose inquiring minds gave light and knowledge to the world.

❧ ☙

Contents

Chapter 1 Victory a Close-Run Thing 1

Chapter 2 Siege of Marseille (Massalia) 13

Chapter 3 Naval Battles.. 17

Chapter 4 Siege on Land 29

Chapter 5 Massalia Capitulates 43

Chapter 6 Attempts to Reclaim its Territories 53

Chapter 7 Survives as an Independent State 59

Bibliography.. 72

Index 79

List of Illustrations

1 Marseille Large Bronze Coin, 210–190 BC 2

2 Marseille Coin, Kent 3rd-2nd Century BC 3

3 British Celtic Potin Coins, Kent 120-100 BC 4

4 Captains, Ancient Greece by Andreas Muller 8

5 Model of Marseille 1st Century BC 11

6 Horn of Lacydon Harbour and City Wall 12

7 Julius Caesar the Siege of Marseille 49 BC 15

8 Naval Battle of Frioul Islands 49 BC 19

9 Roman Arch in Orange, France 23

10 Map of Siege of Marseille 49 BC 30

11 Greek Catapult Aimed at Roman Army 32

12 Vitruvius's Description of the Siege 36

13 Caesar Destroys the Sacred Grove 47

14 Roman Victory of Marseille Coin 48

15 Marseille Minted Coin of Pompey 57

16 Emporion, Spain Three Cities 60

17 Corinthian Helmet 6th Century BC France 70

Illustrations 7, 8, 11, 13 and front cover by Milaskes

ACKNOWLEDGEMENTS

Professor Barry Cunliffe's fascinating lecture in London 2003 on the explorer Pytheas of Marseille: Eleftheria and Parikiaki newspapers for publishing my article of it, which eventually led to these present books.

The cooperation and efficient response from all the numismatic website owners featured in this book is much appreciated.
Marc Breitsprecher, Ancient Imports, ref. SNG 21998, <http://www.ancientimports.com>
CNG <www.cngcoins.com/Coin.aspx?CoinID=115032>
<www.coinarchives.com> Victory over Massalia coin.
Lief Davisson, Davissons Ltd.,www.davcoins.com
Back cover photograph of Marseille Greek Coin by Marie-Lan Nguyen <jastrow@pip.pip.org>

Structurae photograph of Roman Triumphal Arch at Orange France <https://structurae.net/en/structures/orange-roman-arch>

David Holman for photograph and information of Marseille bronze coin found at Tilmanstone Kent UK dated late 3rd early 2nd century B.C.

Professor A. Trevor Hodge for clarification on Apollonides of Massalia during the siege by Julius Caesar and also the permanent gnomon made of masonry in ancient Massalia (Marseille).

D. Garcia for photograph of Greek Corinthian bronze helmet 6th century B.C. found in a grave in Baux-de-Provence, France.

Archaeologists: Marta Santos Retolaza, Director, and Elisa Hernández, Emporion site, Ampurias, Spain for their time and up to date information.

Intercollegiate programmes Birkbeck and Kings College London (KCL): Birkbeck Archaeological Society and KCL Classics Society.

Sue, Rosina, Paul and Mike, Librarians, Institute of Classical Studies Library, Senate House, University of London.

John Mathews, IT Services, Birkbeck, University of London, for help with Microsoft programmes.

CHAPTER 1

VICTORY A CLOSE-RUN THING 49 B.C.

Marseille (Massalia) in France was a city founded in 600 B.C.[1] by the ancient Greeks from their city of Phocaea in Ionia, Asia Minor. Aristotle tells us Marseille was founded for commerce. Strabo writes they made alliance with the then small state of Rome under King Lucius Tarquinius Priscus [2] 616–578 B.C. While the traditional dates of the monarchy are not accurate [3] kings Ancus and Priscus are more historical figures with some leeway on their dates. [4] As Rome became a Republic the Greeks of Marseille (Massalia) maintained their alliance with their navy and army.

Marseilles [Massilia], by the alliance with and power of which we read that Rome itself was more than once supported in moments of danger. [5]

Ammianus Marcellinus, XV.11

Following the Persian invasion of Ionia 545 B.C. Phocaean refugees swelled their Western colonies. Cunliffe suggests the protected area of the Greek city of Massalia (Marseille) of 50 ha had a population 30,000 to 40,000. [6] With the increase in population and territories Massalia founded other cities building up its trading network in France, Spain, Monaco, Corsica and Italy. Greek historian Ammianus Marcellinus records

'Then in subsequent ages, they established no small number of towns, as their strength and resources increased'. [7]

Marseille's trading links to Britain are indicated from British Celtic Potin coins late second century B.C. weight 3–4 grains. The designs are copies of Massalia coins: head of Apollo facing left/reverse: butting bull facing right, above letters MA (for Massalia), [8] similar to this Massalia coin design.

Figure 1. Massalia (Marseille), large bronze, 210–190 B.C. Obverse: laureate Apollo facing left/reverse: butting bull facing right, in exergue ΜΑΣΣΑΛΙΗΤ (MASSALIT), above bow. Size 25.3 mm, weight 11.6 grams.

Copper with an impurity pattern of more cobalt than Nickle Coo>Ni either from Tuscany or from Dartmoor UK was found in some of Massalia's coins [9] which could indicate as well as tin [10] that copper was also exported to Greek Massalia from Britain over 70 years before Julius Caesar invaded Britain. Massalia's explorer Pytheas the astronomer had discovered circumnavigated and named Britain in the 320's B.C. [11] on his voyage to find the origin of valuable Tin and Amber. [12] Diodorus Siculus tells us that Tin was traded by the Britons on a tidal island called Ictis [13] the location of which could be somewhere between Cornwall and the Isle of White.

Figure 2. Late 3rd to early 2nd century B.C. Massalia AE bronze found in Kent at Tilmanstone: laureate Apollo facing left/butting bull facing right, Greek letters for MA(S), courtesy of David Holman.

Figure 3. British Celtic Potin coins, Cantiaci 120-100 B.C. which are copies of Greek Marseille (Massalia) design head of Apollo/ stylised butting bull by courtesy of Davissons Ltd., <www.davcoins.com>.

The Romans had a high opinion of Marseille the Greek city-state on the very periphery of the Greek world from Spain to the Black Sea[14] as expressed by Cicero

> I would be right in saying that in cultures and reliability this city is the superior not only of Greece but probably of the whole world. [15]

Marseille (Massalia) the Greek city-state had a strategic position in keeping the Celts from the 'throat of Italy' and a threat to Rome. During the Roman Civil war 49-45 B.C. Massalia strategic position was between Pompey's seven legions in Spain that now threatened Caesar's rear in Italy. Julius Caesar laid siege to Massalia in 49 B.C.

On Julius Caesar's twelve-day triumph into Rome 46 B.C. we have this testament from Cicero the Roman orator. Cicero mentions in *De Officiis* Marseille (Massalia) special status when comparing Julius Caesar to the dictator Sulla:

> And so, when foreign nations had been oppressed and ruined, we have seen a model of Marseilles [Massilia] carried in a triumphal procession, to serve as proof to the world that the supremacy of the people had been forfeited; and that triumph we saw celebrated over a city without whose help our generals have never gained a triumph for their wars beyond the Alps. [16]

Massalia (Marseille) had supported Pompey the Great against Julius Caesar in the Roman civil war of 49-45 B.C. During 49 B.C. the Massaliotes had received a message from Pompey not to forget the favours he had done them as well as Caesar. On this the Massaliotes

> 'closed their Gates against Caesar and invited over to them the Albici, who had formerly been in alliance with them, and who inhabited the mountains that overhung Massalia'.[17]

Caesar sent for fifteen of the principal persons of Massalia (Marseille) and used several arguments to persuade them to change. Their reply was revealing for the position of a loyal ally for whom to support when civil war breaks out. Reporting to their countrymen the deputies carried the reply,

That they understood that the Roman people was divided into two factions: that they had neither judgement nor abilities to decide which had the juster cause; but that the heads of these factions were Cnieus Pompey and Caius Caesar, the two patrons of the state: the former of whom had granted to their state the lands of the Volcae Arecomici, and Helvii;[18]

while the other, having conquered the Sallyes, had attached this people to their state and boosted their revenues. Therefore, since the benefits the Massaliots had received were equal, their duty was to render equal goodwill to each, help neither against the other, and not receive either within the city or its harbours.[19]

Dio Cassius the Roman historian writes

'Now the Massaliots, alone of the people living in Gaul, did not cooperate with Caesar, and did not receive him into the city, but gave a noteworthy answer'.

He records the events in a similar order to Suetonius except adding that Massalia would receive both if approached in a friendly manner,

'without their arms, but if it were a question of making war, neither of them'.[20]

Consistent with these views Lucan also writes the reply of the Greeks in his epic poem on the Civil War *Pharsalia*:

> And now, if you seek triumphs from an unknown sphere,
>
> our hands are ready, pledged to foreign battles.
>
> But if in discord you plan deadly battle-lines
>
> and ill-omened conflicts, to your civil war we give
>
> our tears and our withdrawal. Let sacred wounds be handled
>
> by no alien hand.[21]

A virtue that was very important to the Romans was *fides* (trust, reliance, faith). Lucan's main theme in his epic civil war poem *Pharsalia* shows it was only Massilia that retains its political *fides* to the end unlike others who crumbled.[22]

Figure 4. Captains by artist Andreas Müller in Braun and Schneider, *Historic Costumes in Pictures*, Plate 3 Ancient Greece: series 1861-90 and reissued by Dover Publications, 1975

'Now the Greek city gained this eternal glory'
(Lucan, III. 388–393)

Because of Caesar's quick movement towards Rome Pompey needed more time to raise his Legions and decided Rome could not be defended with what he had. Pompey the Great and most of the Roman Senate abandoned Italy and made for Greece in which to organise the war against Caesar. His plan was a naval blockade of Italy and to trap Caesar between two great armies namely the seven legions in Spain under three Legates and the forces he was assembling from the Romans and allies in the eastern part of the empire.[23] Caesar's claim was that he was defending the sacred office of the Tribunes, (Mark Antony and Quintius Cassius), whose power had now been reduced by Pompey and the Senate, and therefore he was upholding the constitution. Caesar's Thirteenth Legion 'shouted they were ready to defend their general and the tribunes from harm'.[24]

Though Pompey was now with the Senate he had been accused in the past, by Cato the Younger, of 'promoting anarchy to achieve monarchy'.[25] When the Roman Senate had voted a public thanksgiving of twenty days for Caesar during his Fourth Campaign and first invasion of Britain, Cato the Younger declared that Caesar ought to be given up to the Usipetes and Tenchtheri to atone for his treachery in seizing the sacred persons of their ambassadors.[26] L. Domitius Ahenobarbus was Caesar's enemy and he also called for Caesar's prosecution for his consulship, 'which was supposed to be contrary both to the omens and the laws'. When Domitius was consul he had tried to deprive Caesar of the army.[27] In spite of the unprecedented honours the threat of prosecution when Caesar had finished his commission and became a private citizen, and no longer covered by immunity, was one of the main causes in his refusing to give up the army and march on Rome. On the 7 January 49 B.C. the Roman senate had ordered Caesar to hand over his ten legions to a new Governor.[28]

'By intrigue and cabal' Domitius was appointed Caesar's successor and at the beginning of the Civil War he had been captured at Corsinium by Caesar dismissed and released.[29] Once he was free L. Domitius Ahenobarbus as Caesar's successor, the Governor of Gaul, had requisitioned seven ships from 'private owners' at Igilium and Cosa [30] on the Etrurian coast.[31] The crews for the ships were 'manned with slaves, freedman, and tenant-farmers of his own'.[32] He sailed straight to Massalia and arrived as the legal Governor of Gaul appointed by the Senate and by that position a representative of the officially elected Roman government. Just ahead of Domitius a Massaliote delegation of young nobles had arrived back from Rome having been instructed by Pompey as he was leaving Rome to remember the earlier favours he had done to Massalia and not to be swayed by the recent favours they had received from Caesar. 'The people of Massalia accepted these instructions and closed their gates to Caesar': imported all the corn from the surrounding countryside and their forts: opened the armouries: 'repairing the walls, the fleet, and the gates'.[33]

Caesar summons 'the Fifteen' (cabinet) from Massalia urging 'the Massaliotes to follow the lead of the whole of Italy, rather than humour the wishes of a single man'. After the delegation reported back to Massalia what he said they returned and informed Caesar they made a decision on 'Public Authority' basically to favour neither Pompey or Caesar as they owed much to both equally for the favours done to their city-state and would therefore remain neutral.[34] Caesar writes that negotiations were still proceeding when Domitius sailed into the harbour and 'being placed in charge; he was granted supreme military command.'[35]

Figure 5. A model of the ancient Greek city of Massalia (Marseille) in the Musée d'Histoire Marseille. On left is the big natural harbour with narrow defendable entrance. On the right is the Horn of Lacydon, at the end is by the double gatehouse and the road to Italy. Above the Horn are the ship sheds. At the top are The Frioul Islands and the Mediterranean.

Figure 6. Massalia, foreground the line of the harbour wall of the Horn of Lacydon facing the ancient Greek city with base of a tower on the left and the city walls remains on the right. The Horn ends a few yards to the right and next to the main road to the city through a double gatehouse.

CHAPTER 2

SEIGE BY JULIUS CAESAR

Suetonius writes that Pompey the Great had consulted his friends 'in what manner he should treat neutrals that regarded indifferently both sides of the contest, he [L. Domitius Ahenobarbus] was the only one who proposed that they should be reckoned as enemies and proceeded against accordingly'.[36] Unfortunately for Massalia, who wanted to remain neutral, it was Domitius who arrived as Governor of Gaul and with his extreme views. One may hazard a guess that he had given Massalia no choice of staying neutral. If you are not with us, you are against us? They were either Caesar's or Pompey's enemies? Massalia's ruling aristocrats had been conservative in their outlook and siding with the lawful government of Rome would presumably have come more naturally to them when the time came to make a decision

Domitius ordered the Massaliotes to collect all the boats and grain in the area to be ready in case of a siege. Lucan the Roman poet wrote:

> Now the Greek city gained this eternal glory,
>
> well deserving mention, that, not compelled or prostrated
>
> by sheer terror, it checked the headlong rush of war
>
> raging through the world and when Caesar seized all else at once
>
> it alone took time to be defeated. What an achievement, to detain the Fates. [37]

Though Massalia had tried persuasion and neutrality Lucan recalls their long alliance with Rome, in their reply to Caesar,

> 'That Massalia has always shared your people's fates in foreign wars is attested by every age included in the Latin annals'.[38]

The Greek warriors ended their speech on a resolute note

> 'this people is not afraid to endure for the sake of freedom the ordeal of Saguntum besieged by Punic warfare'.[39]

Figure 7. Julius Caesar the Siege of Marseille 49 BC

This provoked Caesar into sending three legions against Massalia.[40] Carter suggests it was the VI, X, and XIV under Trebonius's command. Later one if not three was replaced by the VII, XII, and XIII, as the XIV went off to Ilerda to join Fabius's three legions.[41] Cassius Dio wrote that 'For Caesar had persisted in his attempt for some time to capture them easily, and regarding it as absurd that after vanquishing Rome without a battle he was not received by the Massaliotes'.[42] He had twelve ships built at Arelate (Arles) in thirty days under the command of Decimus Brutus.[43] Brutus's flagship during his campaign against Massalia was a 'six' with towers and doubled-manned three-oared system '360 oarsmen to man the twelve oar files (30 in number) and entailed 180 oars'.[44] Once the twelve ships had arrived Caesar 'put Decimus Brutus in command of them and left his deputy Gaius Trebonius to take charge of the assault on the city'.[45] Caesar himself made for Spain.[46]

Rowland writes that Massalia (Marseille) possessed a staff of trained engineers/architects and was 'one of the leading cities in siege craft' [47] being well stocked in armaments.[48] Massalia was under siege from April to September 49 B.C. and Caesar victorious took control of the city. This was the city's first defeat in 551 years since it was founded. Earlier the arrival at Massalia of a few ships from Pompey the Great had given much 'hope and enthusiasm' [49] after a defeat at sea. At first the Greeks thwarted all Roman efforts and attacks on land which was interspersed by two naval battles to break Caesar's blockade and control of the sea around Marseille.

CHAPTER 3

NAVAL BATTLES

Clerc [50] questions Massalia's admiral Parmeno's strategy or lack of it? Caesar hurriedly had twelve warships built at Arelate (Arles) in thirty days. These ships had to sail down the River Rhône or along the Marius Channel to Fos to enter the Mediterranean. Clerc said it was 'absolutely incomprehensible' [51] as to why the fleet of Massalia under Parmeno did not go on the attack and blockade Caesar's ships from reaching the Mediterranean. What were the factors in the context of the time? Was Parmeno hampered by the Roman Governor Domitius? Did Domitius or Parmeno know Caesar was building ships? Was there overconfidence? Was Massalia's fleet so run down they needed the time to bring their ships up to scratch?

Yet in the thirty days Caesar built twelve new warships Massalia seemingly did not have access to obtaining new timbers and probably used what was available in the city? Perhaps they were able to get some timber elsewhere by sea while their city was blockaded by Caesar's legions on land until they were also blockaded by sea when Brutus arrived with Caesar's twelve warships. It is possible that Caesar had detachments covering strategic parts of the coast preventing Massalia from landing and foraging. The Romans also attacked Massalia's colonies of Olbia and St. Blaise that year. [52] Once Decimus Brutus had arrived and started his naval blockade Parmeno went on the attack by the Frioul Islands outside Massalia.

The Battle of Frioul

Though the Massaliotes and their allies the Albici fought with valour Parmeno lost nine out of seventeen warships at the Battle of Frioul. While the Greeks fought skillfully giving the Romans the run around, Decimus Brutus worked out a tactic to his own advantage, which was to use his ships like dry land, a platform on which to fight. Lucan writes:

Then Brutus says to his helmsman sitting in the ensign-bearing

stern: "Why do you let the battle-lines range across the deep

and compete with them in manoeuvres on the sea? Now join battle

and present our vessels' sides to the Phocaean prows."

He obeyed and offered his boats sidelong to the enemy.

Then every ship which attacked Brutus' timbers

stuck captive to the one hit, defeated by its own impact,

while others are held fast by grappling-irons and smooth chains

or tangled by their own oars: the sea is hidden and war stands still. [53]

Caesar tells us that the Romans defeated the naval skills and speed of the Massaliotes by the use of grappling hooks to bring the ships together, boarding and close quarter hand to hand fighting. [54] Lucan describes the siege of Massalia: this one of the two Massaliotes' naval battles: and the graphic fates of their sailors Catus, Lycidas, Tyrrhenus, Argus, Telo, and Gyareus. [55] Suetonius mentions briefly a sea fight at Massalia with a Roman Acilius rivalling the feat of the Greek hero Cynegirus.[56]

Figure 8. The Battle of the Frioul Islands, Marseille 49 B.C.

Massalia rebuilt its fleet after the naval Battle of Frioul. Caesar mentions that the authorities had 'repaired old ships' brought out of the ship sheds to bring up to 'its previous size'. They added fishing boats, which 'they had decked to keep the oarsmen safe from the impact of missiles. All these they manned with archers and artillery'.[57] Pompey sent Nasidius with a fleet of sixteen ships, amongst them a few warships, from Dyrrachium (plus one Nasidius took from his surprise landing at Messana on the way), to help Lucius Domitius and the Massaliotes'.[58]

The Battle of Tauroention

Nasidius sent one ship secretly to Domitius and the Massaliotes to inform them of his arrival and together with his fleet to try for another battle against Brutus's fleet. Caesar comments,

> ... they embarked with no less courage and confidence then they had before their previous battle, spurred on by the tears and entreaties of the older men, the women, and the girls, who all begged them to help the city in its hour of crisis. It is a common failing of human nature to be more confident in strange and unprecedented circumstances, as happened on that occasion; for Nasidius' arrival had filled Massilia with hope and enthusiasm. [59]

Waiting for a favourable wind Domitius's ships and the Massaliote fleet sailed out 'and reached Nasidius at Tauroeis, (Tauroention, Le Brusc, near Toulon) which was a fortified outpost of Massilia'. There 'they got their ships ready and for a second time prepared themselves mentally for battle and discussed their plans [60] ... All these they manned with archers and artillery' and by fitting catapults in the battle with Decimus Brutus.[61] Brutus hurried to the same spot with an increased number of ships, Brutus's 12 ships plus the six captured from Massalia previously which he had repaired.[62] Caesar writes 'At the same time a great hail of missiles thrown from the smaller boats caused many injuries to our men who were unprepared, encumbered, and taken by surprise'.[63]

'From Trebonius' Camp and every piece of high ground it was easy to look over the city'.[64] The population in Massalia were observed that those in the temples were prostrate and others on the battlements with uplifted hands, praying to heaven to grant them victory. Those on the ships were from their 'best known families, together with their most distinguished citizens in every period of life, all of whom had received a personal summons and earnest appeal for service'.[65]

Caesar notes the skill of the Massaliote captains. When a Roman ship grappled and held a Massaliote ship, all the other Massaliote ships came to its assistance. Their allies the Albici fought courageously in the hand-to-hand fighting and the hail of missiles from the Massaliote ships caused many injuries to Brutus's ships. By contrast Caesar had little good to say about Massalia's Roman ally Nasidius and his ships, they 'were useless'.[66]

On the left the squadron of Nasidius withdrew out of the action intact, leaving the Massaliotes' squadron. Massalia's Navy was defeated a second time.[67] Caesar thought little of the efforts of Nasidius for he writes

> Nasidius' ships, however, were useless and quickly withdrew from the fighting; no sight of native land, no exhortations of families and friends forced them to risk their lives. And so none of them were lost; from the Massiliot fleet five were sunk, four captured, and one escaped with Nasidius' squadron; these latter all sailed off to Nearer Spain.[68]

One of the surviving ships went back to Massalia to relay the news of the defeat. 'A wail of lamentation ensued, that one might have thought the town had at that very moment been carried by assault'.[69]

In spite of this the Massaliotes continued their efforts with dogged determination in the defence of their city. In his book *Civil War*, Caesar wrote that he thought Massalia's confidence had been 'too great' and Pompey's ships had not proved useful in the battle.

Following the victory Brutus did not force an entry into the harbour with his ships. His forces were not enough once they would have landed and could be repelled. He remained content to continue to blockade the port.[70] While the city continued to live and fight their store of food and armaments would be reduced daily.

While it is thought that the Roman triumphal arch at Orange (Arausio) was built in the reign of Augustus Caesar to commemorate the overall conquests in Gaul of the Second Gallic Legion and no particular battle, Liberati is of the opinion that among the several scenes portrayed [71] included a naval trophy commemorating Julius Caesar's victory at Massalia (Marseille).[72]

Figure 9. Roman Arch, Orange (Arausio), France, one of several scenes depicting military and naval battles.
Photograph by permission of renovators Structurae
<https://structurae.net/en/structures/orange-roman-arch>

Massalia's Commanders 49 B.C.

As no documents survive from Massalia itself we fortunately have a reference in Roman sources that the Massaliote land forces were commanded by Apollonides and the navy by Parmenon, [73] and his replacement Hermon. Professor Hodge [74] has this reference from Cornutus Scholiast to Lucan. [75]

This reference mentioned that the Massaliotes had one person Apollonides[76] as a 'praetor'. Praetor is translated for stratigos (army leader, general).[77] Clerc suggests this was combining the offices of a Magistrate and Commander of the land and naval forces in the siege against Julius Caesar 49 B.C.,

Le général qui commanda les forces de terre fut Apollonidès, qui n'était autre que le Président de la Commission des Trois, et par conséquent du Consiel des Six-Cents, et le commandant de la flotte fut Parménon.[78]

'The general in command of the land forces was Apollonides, and also the President of the Commission of the Three, and consequently Consul of the Six Hundred, and Commander of the fleet of Parmenon'.

Apollonides would have overall command of the defence forces but also over the Government of Massalia.[79] The translation of Strabo does not mention any person in the government of Massalia higher than the Three except in the footnote of H. L. Jones.[80] The same edition is on the Perseus website but without Jones's footnote. I did see at the Museum of History in Marseille illustrated on display boards the political structure of ancient Greek Massalia based on Strabo's description. At the top they write after the 600 senators and above them the council of 15, *'L'un des Trois. Devient le premir magistrat de la cité pendant un an, et donne son nom à l'anneé en cours.* It would seem that above the Three there could have been a premier/supreme commander though this may have been a position enacted only in times of war? Our very brief knowledge comes from a Roman source Cornutus Scholiast to Lucan, III. 375 and 524 from the tenth century A.D. manuscript *Commenta Bernensia* (in Bern, Switzerland):

Massiliam autem aduersus Caesarem defensauit praetor Apollonides, urbi qui praefuit, classi autem Parmeno. [81]

After Massalia's first naval defeat by Decimus Brutus at the Battle of the Frioul Islands Parmeno is replaced by Hermon in command of Massalia's Navy at the Battle of Tauroention (Le Brusc, near Toulon):

dux Gr[a]ecorum Parmeno nauali bello aduersus Brutum fuit prima pugna, sed sequenti, id est hac qua aput Tauronescum dimicatum est, Hermon ei substitutus est, quia Parmeno prius [rem] male gessisset. Hac pugna a Dirracio Lucius Nasidius, auxilo [missus] Massiliensibus, uictus Hispaniam petit. [82]

Massalia's Fleet

How large was the fleet of Massalia? Why at the time of Caesar's and Pompey's civil war were Massalia's fleet so run down and a force was hurriedly patched together from a variety of old ship from their ship sheds? No matter how wealthy a city-state the cost of financing and maintaining ships, the wages of the crew, armaments, keeping the ships in a seaworthy condition are always under pressure in times of peace. The need for a fleet seems an unnecessary expense when there is no immediate threat anymore. Rather like the dominance of the British Navy in first half of the 1900s. Britain ruled the waves. Having won the First World War, of course not alone 'it goes without saying' but in consideration one should 'say it' otherwise a bias or false impression occurs from one's own point of view that certainly was not meant. So more accurately-Britain together with its Empire, Dominions and Allies that included France and its Empire, Russia, Serbia, Montenegro, Japan, Italy, Greece, the U.S.A. (1917-18) and 28 other countries, won the First World War 1914–18. This became known as 'the war to end all wars' where it was thought afterwards that due to the incredible loss of human life no one would be so stupid as to go to war again. However when one society becomes enlightened another is in a primitive and threatening state before it too hopefully develops better human relations. It is an unfortunate blight on humanity that all do not achieve an enlightened view at the same time. Then another generation seemingly having learnt nothing from the past starts the cycle again. In this view of history human progress is painfully slow and held back by temporary regressions. Can the human race ever learn from its mistakes? One must fervently hope so to avoid its own destruction.

The Allies mood to make Germany pay reparations for the war had repercussions. In a defeated country, Germany, with a humiliating peace treaty, economic disasters and runaway inflation fuelled resentment and revenge. Whereas in the country of the non-occupied victor Britain, anti-militarist movements were active such as The No More War Movement and the Peace Pledge Union. This saw the running down of its own armed forces i.e. The London Naval Treaty [83] to the point when Britain found another war approaching they were not militarily ready to meet it and in 1935 increased spending on defence to counter the German threat of rearmament.[84] The similarity to Massalia would be that the threat to its security was thought no longer there.[85] Therefore no need for the expense to maintain a fleet of warships and that the fleet of Massalia became run down while they still had commercial shipping for trade.

Strabo writes, 'And in their citadel are set up great quantities of the first fruits of their victories, which they captured by defeating in naval battles those who from time to time unjustly disputed their claim to mastery of the sea.' Many centuries later with the Roman dominance of Gaul, Massalia was free to pursue arts and develop training schools in the art of speaking and philosophy. In Strabo's time Massalia was still skilled in making navigational instruments and ships equipment.[86]

As the Celts in the interior of Gaul had been conquered by Roman expansion [87] particularly by Pompey the Great and Julius Caesar the threat of the Celts on land and also pirates at sea vanished and with it the need for a big navy by Massalia. This climate of peace lasted until 49 B.C. when Pompey and Caesar opposed each other and a Roman civil war began. Massalia's naval force was not only unready but had to be patched together from even old ships. Being blockaded on land they had no access to the forest for timber. A total of seventeen ships were hurriedly made ready once Massalia had changed from being neutral into joining Pompey's side when Domitius, the Roman Governor, sailed into Massalia while talks were going on with Caesar and would also have put pressure on them to make a choice.[88]

As Pompey actually had 500 ships [89] against the two fleets Caesar had built in the Adriatic and Tyrrhenian Sea [90] it could seem to a city-state that lived traded and supplied itself mainly by the sea that on balance Pompey had the advantage. Pompey could control the Mediterranean and supplies to Massalia (Marseille) if they were blockaded on the landward side by Caesar's legions. The sudden arrival in Massalia of Domitius's ships with Domitius the legal Roman Governor of Gaul [91] replacing Caesar [92] would have made a great impact, a physical link to Pompey and his naval control of the Mediterranean; as well as Domitius's intolerant views on 'neutrals'; [93] that must have influenced the decision of Massalia's government.

Pompey never used his navy to its potential [94] only once sending, under Nasidius, sixteen ships from Dyrrachium to help Massalia. Pompey's strategy was to use his great fleet to stop corn ships from reaching Italy and to patrol the East Mediterranean protecting supplies to his own forces.[95] Nasidius instructed the Massaliote Navy to meet him at Tauroention (Le Brusc). On engaging the twelve ships Caesar had hurriedly made at Arelate (Arles) Nasidius withdrew his ships and left the Massaliotes to it. This defeat at the Battle of Tauroention had won for Caesar control of the sea around Massalia. However devastating this was Massalia put renewed determination in defending the city by land with Apollonides in command.[96]

Their city had never been defeated in all its 550 years and Pompey's navy still had overwhelming superiority in numbers. In hindsight Pompey could have broken the siege and relieved Massalia but never did. The fact that the city of Massalia held out for six months must have astonished everyone considering the speed in which Caesar had conquered in more complicated campaigns like the siege at Alesia in seven weeks. Lucan wrote of Massalia:

> Fearless of Caesar and his arms they stood,
>
> Nor drove before the headlong, rushing flood;
>
> And while he swept whole nations in a day,
>
> Massilia bade th' impatient victor stay,
>
> And clogged his rapid conquest with delay.[97]

CHAPTER 4

SIEGE ON LAND

Caesar had left his legate Gaius Trebonius in charge of the siege [98] and went to Spain to remove the threat of Pompey' Legions at his back.[99] Caesar had said, 'he was going against an army without a captain, and would return thence against a captain without an army'.[100] Marcus Varro in Further Spain had made no move against Caesar (being on good terms with him and Pompey) but hearing of Caesar being held up at Massilia; and that Petreius's army had joined Africanus's army; and Caesar's problem of food supplies at Ilerda, he made a levy to bring his two legions up to strength. Varro 'also requisitioned a quantity of grain to send to Massilia and also to Africanus and Petreius'. He had 'ten warships' built at Gades and many more at Hispalis.[101] Varro surrendered to Caesar when one of his legions went over to Caesar's side.[102]

Caesar's camp at the siege of Massalia was across the marsh at the site of the present railway station Gare St. Charles. This hill was higher than those in Massalia and had a commanding view into the city. The citadel of Massalia was on the hill at the Butte des Moulins.[103]

The peculiarities of Massalia's terrain allowed the Massaliotes to dig down behind their own walls to a greater depth than the town-ditch and 'the miners [Romans] emerged into the open'. The Massaliotes ingeniously were able to flood Roman tunnels trying to undermine the walls from a specially constructed reservoir.[104]

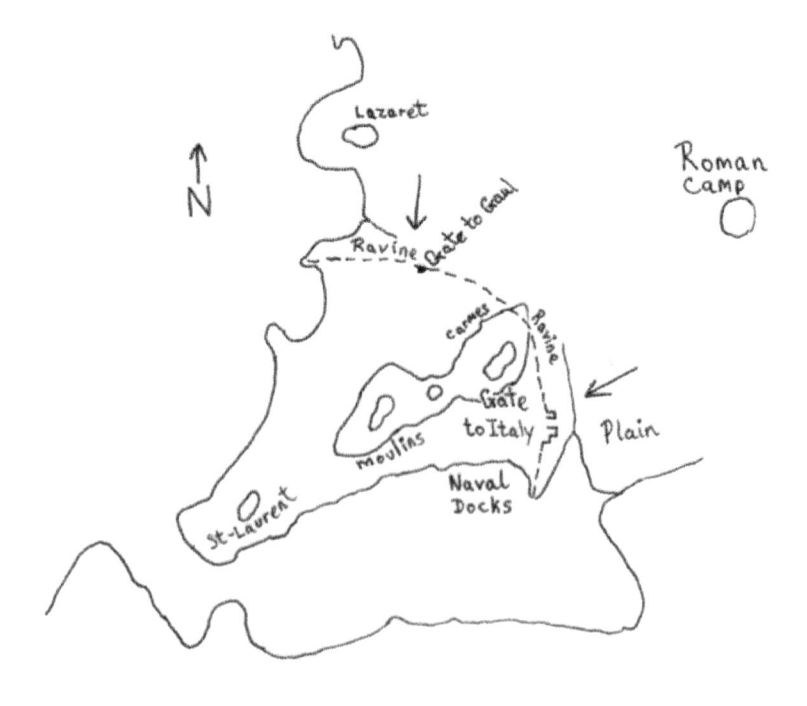

Figure 10. The Siege of Massalia 49 B.C. Massalia was protected by the sea, marshes, ravines, high walls and towers. Arrows indicate the two main areas of attack by Julius Caesar and his Legate Trebonius in addition the Romans tunnelled thirty mines to the city walls.

Massalia's artillery was formidable and its arsenal well stocked Caesar writes 'so great was the store of every sort of military equipment long held in the town, and so great the mass of artillery, that no siege screens of woven osier could possibly resist them'. [105] No light shields could stand up to the artillery and the Massaliotes used palintone engines for shooting large bolts with devastating force.

Caesar records that

> 'Twelve-foot shafts, sheathed with metal points and fired from the large catapults, would drive into the earth after passing through four layers of hurdles'.[106]

> *Asseres enim pedum XII cuspidibus praefixi atque hi maximis ballistis missi per IV ordines cratium in terra defiebantur.* [107]

Figure 11 Greek catapults aimed at Julius Caesar's Roman Army

Coverage illustrated in Lawrence book is based on nine catapults per tower and three either side on the city wall. Therefore six towers 100 yards apart=54 catapults for that section. The added cross-fire must have been devastating.[108]

Evidence of the siege was found at Massalia at the Plaine du Port [109] with stone balls fired at the city wall by the Romans and sling bullets. Lucan records that the Massaliote Tyrrhenus lost his sight when hit on the temple by a sling bullet when he looked up not wishing to miss any of the engagement but probably was exposed when aiming a ballista.[110]

Caesar's Legate Trebonius built 'a siege ramp, siege sheds, and towers against the town in two places'.[111] Trebonius decided to attack Massalia from the following two places. One near the port 'Plaine du Port' by the Gate to Italy, and the other near to the Gate to Gaul and Spain on the north side of the city by the Fabourg suburb.[112] The citadel itself was difficult to attack due to a deep valley/ravine in front of it. The siege ramp Trebonius had constructed was 80 feet high.[113] Julius Caesar wrote that on the arrival of a siege tower at the city wall,

> Panic stricken by this sudden reverse the defenders used crowbars to bring up the largest pieces of stone they could, and tipped these forward off the wall on to the gallery. The strength of the timber stood up to the impact, and everything that fell on the pitched roof of the gallery slid off. Seeing this, the defenders changed their plan. They set light to barrels full of pitch and pine-shavings and rolled these from the wall on to the gallery. The barrels spun along it and rolled off, and when they reached the ground they were pushed away from the sides of the structure with forks and poles.[114]

Vitruvius (Marcus Vitruvius Pollio) was a Roman architect and engineer of the first century B.C. He uses in his book the example of Massalia to show that it is the clever architects who win the battles and not just the machines of war. The books were written to Julius Caesar to persuade him to give Vitruvius a position of employment. From the details given by Vitruvius he may have been at the siege himself and points out to Caesar just how well the Massaliotes nearly defeated all the Roman efforts. He shows it was a much more close-run thing than Caesar actually records in his own book *Civil War*. Here Vitruvius describes the siege of Massalia in his *Ten Books on Architecture*:

The Romans were pushing forward more than thirty mines, the people of Massilia, distrusting the entire moat in front of their wall, lowered it by digging it deeper. Thus all the mines found their outlet in the moat. In places where the moat could not be dug they constructed, within the walls, a basin of enormous length and breadth, like a fish pond, in front of the place where the mines were being pushed, and filled it from wells and from the port. And so, when the passages of the mine were suddenly opened, the immense mass of water let in undermined the supports, and all who were within were overpowered by the mass of water, and the caving in of the mine.[115]

Again, when a rampart was being prepared against a wall in front of them, and the place was heaped up with felled trees and works placed there, by shooting at it with the ballistae red-hot iron bolts they set the whole work on fire. And when a ram-tortoise had approached to batter down the wall, they let down a noose, and when they caught the ram with it, winding it over by a drum turning a capstan, having raised the head of a ram, they did not allow the wall to be touched and finally they destroy the entire machine by glowing fire-darts and blows of the ballistae. Thus by such victory, not by machines but in opposition to the principle of machines, has the freedom of states been preserved by the cunning of architects.[116]

Figure 12. Siege of Massalia 49 B.C. Roman strategies and Greek counter measures based on Vitruvius's descriptions.

The Massaliotes' artillery had been formidable at the beginning of the siege but once the Romans got close to the city wall the front of the catapults could not be lowered down enough [117] to be as effective 'due to the shortness of the range'.[118] Lucan describes the predicament in his epic poem *Pharsalia*:

> But greater was the force of Greek weapons against the Roman
> bodies, because the lance was thrown not by arms
> alone but shot by the taut whirl of the ballista;
> it comes to rest only after passing through more than one body;
> it opens up a path through armour and through bones and
> speeds away,
> leaving death behind: after dealing wounds the weapon still
> moves onwards.
> But whenever a stone is shot by the thong's
> enormous force, like the rock severed
> from the mountain-top by age assisted by the winds' blast,
> it crushes everything in its path, not merely killing
> the pounded bodies but pulverizing entire limbs and blood
> alike.
> But when courage approaches the enemy walls, shielded
> by the dense-packed tortoise—the front line carrying
> overlapping shields, with shield-boss held out to protect the
> helmet—
> then missiles which, when shot from distant point, had
> damaged them before

now fall behind them. And for the Greeks it is no easy task to steer the throw or alter the range of the machine made to hurl its weapons far; [119]

Julius Caesar relates the events of undermining the city wall using a gallery:

Meanwhile under the gallery the soldiers were levering away the lowest stones which formed the foundations of the enemy tower. Our side protected the gallery by firing javelins and artillery bolts from the brick tower, so that the enemy were driven from their wall and towers and given no real chance of defending the wall. By now a good number of stones had been removed from under the adjacent tower, and when suddenly a part of it collapsed and the rest of it in consequence was on the point of doing so, the enemy, terrified by the thought of a sack of their city, all poured out of the gate, unarmed and with the sacred ribbons of suppliants tied around their foreheads, stretching out their hands for mercy to the officers and army.[120]

Caesar's officers received envoys from Massalia asking for a truce:

> They saw that their city was taken, that Caesars' siege works were complete, their own tower undermined, and that they were therefore ceasing their defence. [They said] nothing could happen to hinder Caesar from destroying the city utterly when he arrived, if they did not do exactly what he ordered. They explained that if their tower should collapse completely the [Roman] soldiers would not be able to be held back from bursting into the city in the hope of booty and destroying it. This and much more of the same type- given that they were educated men—was uttered with great pathos and lamentation.[121]

The Roman Officers grant a truce [122] while awaiting the arrival of Caesar [123] and the Greeks use the time to make an attack and aided by the wind destroy with fire the siege works.[124] Dio writes that it was the Romans who had broken the truce. Massalia 'sent out Domitius out of the harbour secretly and caused such injuries to these soldiers, who attacked them in the night in the midst of a truce'.[125] Probably the thought of a settlement after a long siege with no booty had prompted the Romans soldiers into breaking the truce? After nearly six months of siege risking danger and one's comrades being injured or killed the thought of a settlement with no rewards must have angered the ordinary Roman soldiers.[126] Caesar 'had sent the most strict instructions to Trebonius not to let the city be taken by force'. He records that the soldiers at the time of the first truce were threatening to kill all the adults, 'and were with difficulty restrained from bursting into the city, being much annoyed because it was apparently Trebonius's fault that they were not masters of the town'.[127]

Though losing months of work in just a few hours the Romans got over this setback. 'Trebonius began to take his losses in hand and make them good',[128] his soldiers proved resilient and resourceful. As all the wood surrounding Massalia 'far and wide' had been used up by the Romans they decided to build another ramp 'of a new and unprecedented sort' by laying two brick walls bricks six feet thick instead.[129] The roof was covered in timber, 'wicker hurdles and coated with clay'.[130] They also started to build an effective wall and towers that protected their men. The Massaliotes who had been living off 'old millet and rotting barley'[131] with 'food running critically low' [132] realised that their city wall could eventually be enclosed by the Roman's bastioned wall 'on the landward side'.[133] This Roman wall would be higher and therefore their own would be no longer defendable.

At a distance Massalia's artillery had been formidable and effective for six months. Now the Romans had got close up to the city-walls the Greeks

'realised that owing to the shortness of the range their own artillery, on which they rested their hopes, had become useless'.[134]

The grain Varro had requisitioned in Spain to send by ships to Massalia [135] never arrived and neither supplies or soldiers from Pompey. Now the Massaliotes were

'without hope of assistance from provinces or armies which they had learnt had come under Caesar's control'.[136]

Therefore 'It was these considerations which induced them to fall back once more upon the previous terms of capitulation'.[137]

Domitius the Governor heard of the decision to surrender a few days earlier. Caesar had pardoned many enemies who surrendered to him including Domitius before at Corsinium. Yet so implacable was Domitius to Caesar that he did not surrender himself and so escaped by sailing in 'wild weather' while two accompanying ships turned back to port when confronted by the ships of Decimus Brutus.[138] He eventually joined Pompey at Pharsalia where they fought their final battle against Caesar. Domitius was slain in the battle. [139]

CHAPTER 5

MASSALIA CAPITULATES

Caesar records that 'The Massaliotes, as instructed, brought their weapons and artillery out of the town, took their ships out of the port and the ship-sheds, and handed over the money in their treasury'.[140]

Dio says that when Caesar arrived 'he at that time deprived them of their arms, ships and money, and takes of everything except the name of freedom'. To offset this misfortune Phocaea, their mother-city, was made free by Pompey'[141] and the Roman Senate now at Thessaloniki.[142] Caesar spared the city of Massalia leaving 'two legions there as a garrison and sent the others to Italy, while he himself set off for Rome'.[143] Julius Caesar also had good news when he had come to Massalia after conquering Spain regarding the Consular elections. Though a Praetor could not call an election for a Consul he could propose a law for the appointment of a Dictator and this was done by M. Aemilius Lepidus.[144]

This meant that Caesar could now act legally according to Roman law. When Caesar reached Rome he used his position as Dictator to call Consular elections. He resigned as Dictator after eleven days and was elected Consul for 48 B.C. together with P. Serilius Isauricus.[145]

Appian does not mention the siege in his book *The Civil Wars* probably because Massalia was a foreign independent city but he does mention the city in location to Caesar being there.[146] Appian records that Caesar left for Italy 'About the time Antonius was defeated in Illyria by Octavius who was Pompeius's commander operating against Dolabella', part of Caesar's army in Placentia had mutinied 'on hearing this Caesar hastened away urgently from Massilia to Placentia'.[147] 'Caesar went onto Rome after quelling the mutiny of Placentia, where a terrified people elected him Dictator without any decree of the senate or nomination of a magistrate'.[148] Usually this was proposed by a consul.[149] Earlier that year in a letter dated 25 March 49 B.C. Cicero thought it was illegal for a Praetor to hold consular elections or to nominate a Dictator, 'But if Sulla could arrange for a Dictator to be nominated by an Interrex, and a Master of the Horse, why not Caesar?'[150]

From Caesar's point of view, Massalia had gone back on a promise of neutrality[151] and attacked during a truce[152] though Dio did record the truce was 'broken by the Romans'.[153] Caesar says he was lenient when the city capitulated 'preserving the city more out of respect for its fame and antiquity than on account of any favours it had done to him'.[154]

49 B.C.
- Julius Caesar had led three legions to start the siege of Massalia in April.
- The naval Battle of Frioul (Gaul) took place at the end of May.
- The naval Battle of Tauroention/Tauroentum, Gaul, (Le Brusc) took place at the end of June.
- The siege of Massalia ended with its capitulation at the end of September.[155]

At Massalia's colony at Olbia there is a destruction level dated to the mid-first century B.C. and Professor Hodge surmises this may have coincided with the siege of Massalia by Julius Caesar in 49 B.C. There is a superimposed stratum of Roman occupation with hypocaust and Roman Bath.[156] At St. Blaise thirty-nine large stone catapults-balls weighing between eight to forty pounds have been found in a trench that were fired by Romans around the same time as Julius Caesar's siege at Massalia 49 B.C.[157] This may suggest that Julius Caesar's troops had under siege not only Massalia but also other Massaliote cities like St. Blaise and Olbia either at the same time or at some point during 49 B.C.

In April 49 B.C. Julius Caesar had rapidly built 12 warships at Arelate (Arles), Theline)[158] in thirty days to fight Massalia during the Roman civil war. The town of Arelate was awarded a 'Colona Romana' distinction in 46 B.C. when Caesar gave it most of Massalia's territory and settled his veteran troops there.[159] Arelate had been politically and economically dependent on Massalia. By supporting Caesar and the winning side Arelate now became a rich city 'the Rome of the Gauls' at the expense of Massalia by its geographical position, with roads link from Italy to Spain; a port on the River Rhône; and surrounded by fertile land, which provided military supplies.

Massalia's territory was given away in two pieces. The military city of Frejus (Forum Julii) received the lands to the east, and all the lands to the River Rhône went to Arelate (Arles), the civilian port founded by Caesar in 46 B.C. for his veteran soldiers. Caesar called Arelate 'Colonia Julia Paterna Arelatensis Sextanorum' and here he stationed the VI Legion. Only colonies founded by Caesar himself had the right to use the title.[160] However, mindful of Massalia past friendship and help to Rome, Caesar left Massalia itself independent as a *civitas foederata*.[161] Massalia was allowed to keep Nikaia (Nice), Olbia, the Stoechades Islands and Athenopolis from its former empire.[162]

During Caesar's brief eleven days as Dictator before becoming Consul he appointed Decimus Brutus as Governor of the newly acquired Gaul.[163] Decimus had been the admiral of the Roman fleet at the siege of Massalia by Caesar in 49 B.C. Trebonius as Caesar's Legate in charge of the army at the siege then served as a *praetor urbenis* in 48 B.C. also by favour of Caesar. Later Caesar and Trebonius were dead within a year of each other.

Caesar had earlier destroyed the barbarous ancient sacred grove outside Massalia ('mine is the guilt').

'iam nequis vestrum subverte silvam credite me fecisse nefas'.

where the Gauls groaned at its loss but Lucan has the watching Massaliotes jubilant expecting swift divine aid.

'For who would think that gods are injured without revenge?'

The Massaliotes as religious Greeks must have been perplexed when no divine 'revenge' came to Caesar. His soldiers had been reluctant to commit sacrilege by cutting down the barbarous sacred grove whereas Caesar seized an axe and started chopping saying any guilt and therefore divine punishment would be his ('mine is the guilt') and freeing the soldiers to cut down the grove without blame. While Lucan portrays Caesar as reason and civiliser of barbarism who survives proving superior to superstition he still succumbs to retribution five years later when assassinated. Though whether it was divine retribution or a deadly human reaction to his ambition or one using the other you can judge. [164]

Figure 13 Caesar cuts down the Barbarous Sacred Grove

Julius Caesar's moneyer during the dictatorship was L. HOSTILIVS SASERNA. He was in the office of Triumvir Monetale (IIIVIR).[165] HOSTILIVS issued coins in 48 B.C. from the mint in Rome. One coin is thought to commemorate Caesar's victory over Massalia the year before in Gaul.[166] This now very rare silver Denarius coin shows on the obverse a long haired woman's head possibly a captive or representing Gallia facing right, with a Carnyx (Celtic trumpet with a dragons head) behind.[167] On the reverse is the goddess of Massalia Ephesian Artemis facing standing, with a leaping stag and it seems held by the antlers at the head or right hand on the stag's head, and holding an upright spear in the left hand, with the words L. HOSTILIVS vertically downwards on right, and SASERNA upwards on the left. Weight 3.66 gm.

Figure 14. Silver Denarius coin issued in Rome by Julius Caesar's moneyer L. Hostilius Saserna in 48 B.C. thought to commemorate Julius Caesar's victory in Gaul and Massalia 49 B.C.

We generally view this period in Rome as a struggle of power between Pompey and Julius Caesar but there were also other rivals in that context which set the conditions leading to the Civil War.

The Republic had become unstable with the intense rivalry amongst the senator class for the top positions in the state. Political unrest was due to both Clodius and Milo who being violent men had led rival gangs in street fights in Rome. The rivalry continued several years to when Milo was a candidate for the Consulship and Clodius for the Praetorship.[168] Daily street fights had made it impossible to hold the elections. In one fight the gangs met just outside of Rome and Clodius was killed by Milo in 52 B.C. The Senate took a new measure and made Pompey sole consul to stop the street fighting. Milo was put on trial and Cicero defended Milo but was intimidated. As Cicero started speaking there were yells from Clodius's supporters, which the presence of soldiers did not stop. Plutarch mentions that on seeing so many 'weapons glistening all round the Forum, he [Cicero] was so confounded that he could scarce begin his oration. For he shook and his tongue faltered, though Milo attended the trail with great courage'.[169]

Having lost the case Milo was sentenced to exile and he chose Massalia. He left within a few days and his property sold for one twenty-fourth of its value due to 'large debts'. [170] He took with him many slaves.[171] Milo perhaps chose Massalia in Gaul, as there were many Roman exiles in Epirus and enemies of his.[172]

Milo's Mullets

Cicero sent the speech he had meant to speak at the trail to Milo now in Massalia. Upon reading it Milo replied,

> 'I am glad it was not delivered, for I should then have been acquitted, and never known the delicate flavour of these Massillon Mullets'.[173]

Considering how close he had been to being elected Consul, the top job in Rome, and having got rid of his enemy Clodius, to suddenly now be in exile one could view Milo's comments not that of a lucky chap on holiday, but maybe taking a philosophical view of his situation or perhaps he was being sarcastic even though the Massillon Mullets were extremely good. Dio Cassius writes of Milo:

For he should not be eating such mullets in Massalia (where he had been passing his exile), if any such defence had been made. This he wrote, not because he was pleased with his condition—indeed he made many efforts to secure his return—but as a joke on Cicero, because the orator, after saying nothing useful at the time of the defence, had later composed and sent to him these fruitless words, as if they could then be of service to him.[174]

When Julius Caesar was Dictator for eleven days before becoming Consul again during the Civil War he allowed all exiles to return except Milo.[175] Though Caesar does not mention Milo in his book he would still have been at Massalia when Caesar was there to accept the city's surrender in 49 B.C. during the Civil War and it seems probable that they would have met and more likely interviewed/assessed him? Whatever they may have said determined Caesar's actions in leaving Milo there in exile (no doubt to continue his 'appreciation' of Massalia's Mullets)! He was 'known to be a man of wicked daring' as was evident on his return to South Italy (without permission) to join Caelius in the freebooter rising against Caesar in 48 B.C. where he was killed.[176]

Roman Monarchy

Yet with a number of rivals trying for individual power there was still a very strong Republican support. The conflict of attitudes that fuelled the Roman civil wars was the strong underlying belief and tradition against one man ruling, a monarch, and the vying amongst the senatorial class for the limited top positions in the state. Justin records that

> Such was the principle of hatred towards all monarchs that they had established, evidently because they themselves had had kings who were such that even their names made them blush: shepherds from amongst the Aborigines, soothsayers from the Sabines, exiles from Corinth, slaves from Etruria, captured or bred at home, or—the most distinguished name of them all—the Superbi.[177]

Many kings of Rome had been outsiders and not from the patrician class.[178] Cornell points out that when the Republic was formed its first act was to make people swear never to allow a man to be a king in Rome and legislated against anyone seeking to become a king in the future.[179] More than anything else it was the thought that one of their own should be higher than themselves by championing the needs of the lower classes and getting their political support. King Ancus Marcius had been a patron of the Plebs and King Lucius Tarquinius Priscus canvassed the people and his reforms angered the aristocrats.[180]

Remarkably in the Republic those from the ruling class that made particular efforts to help the poorer classes were then accused of monarchism (*Regnum*) such as Sp. Cassius, Sp. Maelius, M. Manilus Capitolinus and T. Gracchi.[181] It seems to have gone hand in hand that amongst those who hated kingship also feared the lower classes might have an increase in power in Rome because of it. Sharing power met with resistance as it did in not giving Roman citizenship to their Italian allies resulting in the Social Wars 90–89 B.C.

CHAPTER 6

ATTEMPTS TO RECLAIM ITS TERRITORIES

After Julius Caesar's assassination in March 44 B.C. events were becoming precarious as revealed by Cicero in a letter to Atticus on 26 April 44 B.C.:

> if there is going to be a civil war—and that there must be, if Sextus stays under arms, as I know for certain he will—I don't know what we are to do. For now there will be no chance of sitting on the fence, as there was in Caesar's war. For, if this gang of ruffians thinks anyone was rejoiced at the death of Caesar—and we all of us showed our joy quiet openly—they will count him an enemy; and that looks like a considerable massacre. Our alternative is to take refuge in Sextus' camp, or join ourselves to Brutus if we can. [182]

Atticus wrote to his friend Cicero and asked him to restore Massilia's rights. However Mark Antony and his supporters were a power in the Senate. Cicero writes back to Atticus 27 April 44 B.C.:

> But here you are wanting to get back their rights for your neighbours the Massilians, as though we had recovered the republic. Perhaps they might be restored by arms—but how strong our arms are I do not know—by influence they certainly cannot.[183]

After Trebonius had been killed by Dollabella in Smyrna 43 B.C the Senate declared Dollabella an 'Enemy to the Roman people'.[184] Mark Antony wrote a letter with several complaints to the consul Hirtius and propraetor Caesar (Octavian), which included,

> 'You have taken away the veterans' colonies, though planted by law and by decree of the Senate. You are promising to restore to the Massilians what has been taken from them by the laws of war'.[185]

Cicero comments in his *Philippic* against Mark Antony,

> Yet consider whether it is not you that have ruined these veterans who have been ruined, and planted them in a position from which they themselves already feel they will never escape. "You are promising to restore to the Massilians what has been taken away from them by the laws of war". I do not agree as to the laws of war—the argument is more easy than necessary; but notice this point, Conscript Fathers, what a born enemy to this State Antonius is; who so bitterly hates that community which he knows has been always most friendly to this State.[186]

Cicero in speaking to restore Pompeius's dignity and his fortune to his son Pompeius Sextus said,

> in spite of our confirmation and ratification of the acts of Caesar, the son of Cnaeus Pompeius should be able to recover his dignity and the fortune of his father . . . illustrious envoys Lucius Paulus, Quintus Thermus, and Caius Fannius, whose unremitting and steadfast good will towards the State, you have realised, announce that they turned aside to Massilia in order to meet Pompeius, and recognised that he was most ready to go to Mutina with his forces, but feared to offend the veterans [of Caesar].[187]

The veterans of the VI Legion that Caesar had settled at Arles (Arelate) were recalled, up to four years under the terms of their discharge in times of emergencies, by the summer of 44 B.C. They re-joined their legion now part of Lepidus's army encamped by the River Var. [188]

After Caesar's assassination the Senate recalled Pompeius Sextus from Spain and he stayed in Massalia 44–43 B.C. keeping an eye on political developments in Rome while at a safe distance.[189] If Lepidus's legions moved against him he could make a quick exit by sea.

Would the supporters of Pompey, Mark Antony or Octavian gain control of the Senate? Appian wrote that Mark Antony made a surprise proposal to recall Pompeius Sextus from Spain 'and that he should be paid 50 millions of Attic drachmas out of the public treasury for his father's confiscated property'.[190] The Senate approved Pompeius Sextus command of the sea 'with charge of all Roman Ships, wherever situated, which were needed for immediate service'. [191]

Mark Antony was a masterful politician. He already had Amatius put to death by his authority as Consul without trail for making 'perpetual terror' on Caesar's murderers with several fleeing Rome. In doing so Mark Antony temporarily turned the people against himself; but gained the 'delight' of the Senate as the action clearly was to protect Gaius Cassius Longinus and Marcus Junius Brutus. Mark Antony broke up the following protest by Amatius's supporters and had several killed.[192] He won much praise by the Senate and Cicero by this popular move where particularly the Pompeians, Appian records, readily believed 'the Republic would at last be restored' and 'their party successful'.[193]

Clerc writes that Sextus in Massalia made Apollonides the overall Greek Commander of Massalia during the siege by Julius Caesar in 49 B.C. a Roman citizen.[194] The Massalia mint was still active and issued coins for Sextus with his father Pompey the Great on the obverse and the reverse shows a galley with the word NASIDIVS. Nasidius was the admiral in charge of the Roman fleet helping Massalia (Marseille) during the Civil War against Julius Caesar's admiral Decimus Brutus at the two naval battles of Frioul Islands and Tauroention.

Figure 15. Made and issued from Massalia's mint 44–43 B.C. by Pompey's son Pompeius Sextus. Silver Denarius, obverse: Pompey the Great facing right, Trident, Dolphin, inscription Neptune/reverse: a crewed ship, oars and full sail, facing right, inscription NASIDIVS, six rayed star. Weight 3.73 g, 6 h.

Coins could also be used as blatant propaganda. Marcus J. Brutus had coins issued obverse: portraying his head, and around BRVT IMP L PLAET CEST and on the reverse a pileus between two daggers with letters below EID MAR (Ides of March) justifying his murder of Caesar as saving the Republic from a tyrant. Pompeius Sextus issuing a coin with his father's image and his admiral Nasidius would not have endeared himself to Mark Antony, Octavian or the supporters of Caesar.

To get all Caesar's decrees posthumously passed in the Senate Mark Antony had to agree to a decree allowing no prosecution of Caesar's murderers. With the leaders of the colonists also present in the Senate they asked for 'another act special to themselves'. This was also passed 'to secure them in possession of their colonies'.[195] Cassius and Marcus Brutus were still in Rome as city Praetors before taking up their Governorships of Syria and Macedonia respectively. They also 'conciliated the colonists by varying degrees, and among others by enabling them to sell their allotments, the law hitherto forbidding the alienation of the land till the end of twenty years'.[196]

Appian records that Sextus still did not return to Rome but 'taking what ships he found in the harbours, and joining them with those he had brought from Spain, he put to sea'.[197] This may suggest that Massalia also had ships again after their confiscation by Caesar following his siege in 49 B.C. Sextus spent part of 43 B.C. refurbishing his fleet in Massalia.[198] Massalia now full of ships, a hive of industry and fully employed in building and supplies. However the wheel of fortune turned again when Mark Antony, Octavian Caesar and Lepidus formed the Triumvirate and took absolute power with a proscription (death list).[199] Sextus sailed to Sicily and gained possession of the island in 42 B.C.[200] and cut off corn supplies to Rome inducing famine.[201].

Following a temporary peace [202] Sextus won naval battles against Octavian Caesar and exchanged the purple cloak of a Roman commander to that of blue 'to signify he was the adopted son of Neptune'.[203] At this time events were looking hopeful for Massalia (Marseille) with Sextus gaining the upper hand yet the wheel of fortune had not stopped spinning. Finally Octavian beat Sextus at sea and Sextus died later while fighting against Mark Antony's forces on land in Bithynia (in North-West Asia Minor).[204]

CHAPTER 7

SURVIVES AS AN INDEPENDENT STATE

With Lepidus deprived of his province in Gaul and Spain [205] and later deposed of his command; [206] the loss of influence in the Senate of the Pompeians; Marseille (Massalia) having taken the losing side of the Republic and Pompey's cause had little chance of getting their empire back with Octavian and Mark Antony in power.[207] Whichever side was in power neither risked offending the veterans Julius Caesar had planted in Arelate (Arles) or the Roman colony of Fréjus (Forum Julius) who both benefited from the surrounding lands given to them by the division of the Greek Empire of Marseille (Massalia).

Julius Caesar also added a Roman colony to the mixed population of Iberians and Massaliotes in the Marseille colony of Emporion (Ampurias, Spain)[208] to ensure their loyalty. A Roman colony had also been settled at the Phocaean colony of Lampsacus in Asia Minor.[209] Around c.37-27 B.C the Greek city of Emporion and the adjacent Roman city formed the Roman Municipum of Emporiae with both still keeping their separate boundaries.[210]

The Greeks from Marseille founded their colony at Emporion in Spain c.600-575 B.C. at first on the island (1.Paleopolis). Evidence of standardized rectangular buildings from 580 B.C. replaced mud huts.[211] The Iberian Indicetans invited them to build a city on the mainland opposite (2. Neapolis) shared under one constitution.[212] The populations co-existed successfully with the Indicetans and Greeks living in their own halves separated by a wall in which the gate was closed at night. The outer walls of the Neapolis are still impressive with Cyclopean stones at the South Gate.

Figure 16. Emporion, Spain, three separate cities next to each other by the first century B.C.
1. Original Greek Paleopolis on an island: 2. Greek Neapolis on the mainland: 3. Hellenistic Breakwater (remains) originally longer and opposite another extending out from the Paleopolis: 4. Harbour: 5. Roman city: 6. Present day coastline: 7. River Fluvia

At Emporion a very rare find of a Greek catapult (Euthytonon) dating from the 2nd century BC was excavated amongst a hoard of weapons in an arsenal near the South Gate of the Greek Neapolis in 1912. Schraam's full-size reconstruction of this Euthytonon is in the Saalburgmuseum, Bad Homburg, Germany.[213]

After their loss of territories it is thought that Massalia's commercial importance must have declined but archaeological evidence suggests the opposite. There were major new port installations built late first century B.C. (in use until the third century A.D.),[214] and in the city using building stone from Cap Couronne.[215]

One funeral inscription dated to end of the first to beginning of the second century A.D. [216] shows the Roman system of three names *tria nomina* with family name preceded by Roman or name of ancient benefactor to the family. Clerc suggests that the name Titus Pompeius Apollonides found on a funerary stone might possibly be from the family of Apollonides who had been the overall Commander of Massalia in 49 B.C. siege against Julius Caesar.[217] The Greek inscription was found at the necropolis of Carénage outside ancient Massalia: [218]

ΤΙΤΟΣ • ΠΟΜΓΗΪΟΣ
ΑΠΟΛΛΩΝΙΔΗΣ
ΤΙΤΩΦΛΑΟΥΪΩΙ
ΝΕΙΚΟΣΤΡΑΤΩΙ
ΤΩΙΚΑΘΗΓΗΤΗΙ
ΜΝΗΜΗΣ • ΧΑΡΙΝ

Titus Pompeius Apollonides, (erected this gravestone) to Titus Flavius Nicostratus, (his) teacher, as a memorial. [219]

With the consolidation of Mark Antony and the triumvirate upholding dead Caesar's decrees passed in the Senate regarding the settlement of the veterans, (Caesar's veterans were at Arles), all hope was gone for Massalia in getting their territories back, which had been given to those two cities of Frejus and Arles. This marked the end of an era but to be exact only a part of an era. Massalia was still independent but the 'Greek Empire of Marseille' (Massalia) had come to an end though it was allowed to keep and control Nikaia (Nice), Olbia, the Stoechades Islands, and Athenopolis [220] (the location of which is still to be discovered and only conjecture without more evidence as being Saint-Tropez). [221]

However, in trade Massalia's markets were still there, meeting supply and demand in which Massalia was very successful for 550 years. With that experience, contacts in trade, and allowing for costs for hiring other ships until you had your own again Massalia was still in business. That trade continued is archaeologically evident with renewed port installations in the late first century B.C. in use up to third century A.D. Roman traders were also in Massalia and it was now a Roman world and a global market but Massalia maintained its political and commercial independence *civitas foederata* as a Greek city within it: [222]

Pliny the Elder recorded:

'On the coast is Marseilles, founded by the Greeks of Phocaea and now a confederate city'.[223]

at in ora Massilia Graecorum Phocaeensium foederata.

Strabo (64 B.C.–A.D. 24) recorded that Massalia maintained its independence under Rome:

> Both Caesar and the commanders who succeeded him, mindful of their former friendship, acted in moderation with reference to the wrongs done in the war, and preserved to the city the autonomy which it had had from the beginning; so that neither Massilia nor its subjects are subject to the praetors who are sent to the province. [224]

Leading families in Massalia adopted the custom of giving themselves three names in the Roman style. As evident on funerary inscriptions found in Massalia starting with the benefactor of the family and ending with the family name. Trade went on and so did Massalia still trading with its other ex-colonies, not in political or military control but still as the independent Greek city-state of Massalia.[225]

Though its city's treasury had been emptied into Julius Caesar's funds for bribery, triumphs, great civic works and military pay, it would seem that Massalia's citizens own private money had been left alone. Sextus refurbished his fleet there boosting Massalia's economy. Having survived an 'asset stripping' and now without the expense to keep a Greek Army or a Navy, a leaner Massalia could survive economically independent in a Roman world of trade and commerce not only as a cultural university city. Strabo in the first century A.D. reports that they 'were skilled in the making of navigational instruments and ships equipment'.[226] This shows that maritime skills were present and active in an independent Massalia during the following era of the Roman peace-Pax Romana.

Massalia maintained its reputation for Greek culture and learning. Among other schools it was also the home of Agroitas. Here is a story related by Seneca the Elder:

> Agroitas of Marseille [Massalia] produced a much more forceful epigram than the other Greeks declaimers, who brawled in this *controversia* as though they were rivals in love. Now Agroitas had an unpolished technique (which showed he had not frequented the Greeks) and employed vigorous epigrams (which showed he had frequented the Romans). This was the epigram which won applause: "This is where we are at discord in our debauchery: you are debauched and enjoy it; I am debauched and do not." [227]

There was also the School of Moschus the Apollodorean of Massalia.[228] In Strabo's time Massalia 'attracted the most notable of the Romans, if eager for knowledge, to go to school there instead of making their foreign sojourn at Athens'.[229] Among them was Agricola who studied philosophy and later became a Consul of Rome and Governor of Britain. Tacitus (c. A.D. 55–117) the Roman historian gave a good view of Massalia in his book called *Agricola* about his father-in-law:

He was shielded from the snares of sinners not merely by his own good and upright nature but because from the outset of his childhood the home and guide of his studies was Massilia, a blend and happy combination of Greek refinement and provincial simplicity.

I remember how he used himself to tell that in early life he was inclined to drink more deeply of philosophy than is permitted to a Roman and a Senator, had not his mother's discretion imposed a check upon his enkindled and glowing imagination.[230]

There were two good reasons why Massalia had kept its own distinct culture. One was policy and the other geography. Morris points out that the Romans actively retained the Greek identity of Massalia, as a continuing, civilising buffer against the 'barbarians' of Gaul.[231] Justin writes of the civilizing influence of Greek Massalia on its surrounding neighbours.[232] While Bats thought the Greeks affected small and different parts of the populations yet they nevertheless 'prepared the ground for the subsequent acculturation by the Romans'.[233]

Strabo writes that the Celts had begun attending school in Massalia and the Galatae were 'fond enough of the Greeks to write even their contracts in Greek.'[234] Julius Caesar had found in the camp of the Helvetii a census of their population in Greek script.[235] The Nervii had 'six hundred senators' and could this system have been learnt from the government of Massalia?[236] Although Caesar records that the Druids never wrote anything down and memorised their knowledge, he adds 'although in almost all other matters, and in their public and private accounts, they make use of Greek letters'.[237] A Gallo-Greek script was also in use from third century B.C.[238] and by the early first century B.C. Greek script is being used in the upper Rhône valley and Burgundy[239] and continued in Provence after invaded by the Romans to mid-first century A.D. Again we can see a connection between Celts and Greeks through the schools at Massalia.

Geographically Massalia was also able to maintain its own culture and character as it was not on the main road of the Via Domitia,[240] only being reached by a spur off the road from Aix-en-Provence, or even the later Via Julia. The main routes went inland through Arelate (Arles) or Tarascon.[241] Previously there was a rough track near Massalia known as the Via Heraclensis (used by Herakles [Hercules] in his Labours) but unsuitable for 'serious transport' until the Roman Emperor Augustus had constructed the Via Julia c. 13 B.C. further north.[242]

Incidentally Morel mentions 'a Marseillan fact' in the *Geryoneis* as Hercules was saved by an attack of the Ligurians when Zeus made it rain pebbles that correspond to La Crau, a plain covered with pebbles close to Marseilles, east of the Rhône delta[243] and west of the Camargue.[244] Pliny the Elder also mentions a tradition of Hercules fighting battles in this area of the 'Stony Plains'.[245]

Summary

Strategic Massalia undefeated for 550 years was a loyal ally of Rome. Having received land in the past from Pompey and Julius Caesar's conquests Massalia sought to remain neutral in their dreaded Roman civil war 49-45 B.C. Domitius the newly appointed Governor of Gaul representing Pompey and the Roman Senate arrived in Massalia, gaining their aid and the Albici allies to oppose the outgoing Governor Julius Caesar and his support of the Tribunes.

Caesar led three legions against Massalia starting a six-month siege, continued under his legate Trebonius while he made for Spain. Massalia's ingenuity thwarted 30 mines tunneled to the city-walls. After Massalia burned Roman siege equipment, Roman inventiveness made a brick walled ramp and a towered wall. Apollonides was in overall command of Massalia. He had admiral Hermon replace Parmeno after the first naval defeat. Reinforced by 17 ships from Pompey they were defeated by Caesar's 12 ships from Arles and 6 taken before from Massalia. Massalia's artillery was formidable at long range but ineffective once the Romans got close to the wall. Supplies of men from their colonies or Pompey and grain from Varro in Spain never arrived. Rotting food and diminishing stocks led the Greeks to capitulate to Caesar who had returned from success in Spain. Evidence suggests attacks on their colonies of Saint-Blaise and Olbia by the Romans around the same time.

While Caesar stripped Massalia's treasury, ships, arms and territories he left the city itself independent for past support to Rome and 'its fame and antiquity'. Caesar placed a Roman colony at Massalia's colony of Emporion in Spain to ensure its loyalty. After Caesar's murder Massalia attempted to get back all their lands with the support of Hirtius, Octavian Caesar, Cicero and the Pompeian party but were blocked in the Senate by Mark Antony. None wished to offend the veterans who had been settled in Massalia's former territories in Gaul divided between Fréjus and Arles. Hope still remained with the victories of Sextus, son of Pompey, until defeated by Octavian Caesar and Mark Antony.

A century later we find Massalia still in control of Nice, Stoechades Islands, Olbia and Athenopolis from its former empire. Massalia continued as a university city where notable Romans went for education if they did not want to go to Athens. Agricola, Governor of Britain, studied philosophy there in his youth, a place of 'Greek refinement and provincial simplicity'. For the Romans it was useful to have the Greek identity of Massalia as another civilising influence on Gaul.

For a fuller history of Marseille including its colonies and explorers who discovered Britain and gave the name Britain see:

C. Gunstone,. *The Greek Empire of Marseille: Discoverer of Britain, Saviour of Rome,* Silver Shields, 2013
ISBN: 978-1481239660.
The book is available from Amazon in Kindle and paperback.

Postscript

Phocaea founded these colonies in the Western Mediterranean: Herakles Monoikos (Monaco) c 620 BC: Theline (Arles), Aouenion (Avignon) trading centre from 6th century BC (Greek masonry was found at the deepest level in excavations): and Marseille 600 BC.

Phocaea together with Marseille then founded Alalia (Aleria in Corsica) c.565 BC who subsequently founded Hyele (Elea-Velia) c.540 BC the last Greek city established in Italy (Magna Graecia).

Marseille singularly founded, Agathe Tyche (Agde) 580 BC, Antipolis (Antibes), Nikaia (Nice), Olbia (Saint Pierre L'Almanarre, Hyeres) 350 BC, Tauroention (Le Brusc near Toulon) c.300 BC, Emporion (Sant Marti d'Empuries, Spain) c.600-575 BC, Rhodus (Roses, Spain) 4th century BC. There are several more cities listed in the literary record but need archaeological evidence to find their locations i.e. Iberian Kyrene, Athenopolis (Saint-Tropez?), Castrum Marselinum (Cannes?) and Troizen in Italy etc.

Saint-Blaise (6th century BC, several phases, abandoned and repopulated) and Avignon might have been mixed population like Emporion.

Figure 17. Greek Corinthian bronze helmet 6th century B.C. found in a grave in Baux-de-Provence, France. By permission of: D. Garcia, 'Le casque corinthien des Baux-de-Provence' in S. Bouffir and A. Hemary (eds.) *L'occident grec, de Marseille à Mégara Hyblaea*, (Centre Camille Jullian, 2013): 85-90.

ABOUT THE AUTHOR

Christopher Gunstone BA (Hons), ACIM is a historian, archaeologist, and writer. He read Independent Studies at Lancaster University, thesis Origins of the British: and read History and Archaeology at Birkbeck. At fourteen years of age his first experience of excavation was as a volunteer at Reculver Iron Age/Roman fort and discovered a burial in the foundations! As a student at Lancaster he also worked as a museum assistant in charge of the Campbell Legend Exhibition on Lake Windermere. He has had articles published in the London Greek newspapers Eleftheria and Parikiaki, and appeared on TV and Radio. Recently he has been working in London as part of the Foreshore Recording and Observation Group, Thames Discovery Programme (TDP): TDP photographic exhibition at Discover Greenwich, ORNC: and visited several of the archaeological sites featured in this book.

Bibliography

A. Augoustakis, 'Cutting Down the Grove in Lucan, Valerius Maximus and Dio Cassius', *The Classical Quarterly*, vol. 56, No. 2 (Dec, 2006):634-638 <www.jstor.org/stable/4493456>.

Appian, *The Civil Wars*, Book II. 48, trans. J. Carter, Penguin, 1996

Appian The Civil Wars, II, 135, *The Histories of Appian*, Loeb, 1913, <http://penelope.uchicago.edu/Thayer/E/Roman/Texts/Appian/Civil_Wars/2*.html> ['Penelope, University of Chicago' digital library]

D. Baatz, 'Recent Finds of Ancient Artillery', *Britannia*, Vol. 9 (1978), pp. 1-17, Society for the Promotion of Roman Studies, ['JSTOR' journal archive] <https://www.jstor.org/stable/525936>

W. W. Bateson and C. Damon, *Caesar's Civil War,* Oxford, 2006.

M. Bats, 'The Greeks in Gaul and Corsica: the rhythm of the Greek emporion', P. Carratelli (ed.), *The Western Greeks: classical civilization in the Western Mediterranean* (London, 1996): 577–584

P. G. Bilde and J. H. Petersen (eds.), *Meeting of Cultures in the Black Sea Region,* (University of Aarhus, 2008)

Caesar *The Civil War,* Bk. I.35, trans. J. Carter, Oxford's World Classics, 1998

Cicero, *De Officiis,* Bk. II. 8. 28–29, trans. W. Miller, Loeb, 1975,

Cicero, *Letters to Atticus,* vol. 3. 183 (IX.15), trans. D. R. Shackleton Bailey, Harvard University Press, 1999

Cicero, *Pro Milone,* trans. N. H. Watts, Heinemann, 1972

Cicero Philippic, XIII. xv. 30–32, trans. W. Ker, Loeb, 1926

Cicero, *The Speeches: In Catilinam I–IV. Pro Murena. Pro Sulla. Pro Flacco*, trans. C. MacDonald, Heinemann, 1977

H. Cleere, *Southern France: An Oxford Archaeological Guide*, Oxford, 2001

M. Clerc, *Massalia*, 2 vol. .Marseille, 1927–9; (reprint Lafitte, Marseille, 1971) 2

T. J. Cornell, *The Beginning of Rome: Italy and Rome from the Bronze Age to the Punic Wars (c. 1000–264 B.C.)*, Routledge, 1995

B. Cunliffe, *The Extraordinary Voyage of Pytheas the Greek: The man who discovered Britain,* Penguin Books, 2002

S. Dando-Collins, *Cleopatra's Kidnappers: How Caesar's Sixth Legion Gave Egypt to Rome and Rome to Caesar*, John Wiley & Sons, 2005

Dio's Roman History, vol.4. Bk. XLI, trans. E. Carey, Heinemann, 1916

Diodorus Siculus, *Histories*, V.22, *The Library of History of Diodorus Siculus,* vol. 3. Loeb, 1939

M. Fröhner, 'Scolies latines relative a l'histoire et a la topographie de Marseille', *Revue Archéologique*, XVIII, II, (1891): 321-332, Scholiast to Lucan III.524.

R. Gardiner, (ed.), *The Age of the Galley,* Conway Maritime Press, 1995

A. Hermary, A. Hesnard, and H. Tréziny, *Marseille Grecque: La cite phocéenne (600–49 av. J-C),* Editions Errance, 1999

A. Trevor. Hodge, *Ancient Greek France*, University of Pennsylvania Press, 1999

G. H. R. Horsley, *New Documents Illustrating Early Christianity: A Review of the Greek Inscriptions and Papyrii published in 1979*, vol. 4, Macquarie University, 1987

Inscriptiones Graecia, vol. XIV. Appendix, Inscriptiones Galliae, III, Massalia, 2454. Berolini, 1890

P. de Jersey, *Celtic Coinage in Britain,* Shire, 2001

Justin: Epitome of the Philippic History of Pompeius Trogus, 43.4.1, trans. J. C. Yardley, Scholars Press Atlanta, GA, 1994

G. P. Kelly, *A History of Exile in the Roman Republic,* Cambridge, 2006

W. E. Klingshirn, *Caesarius of Arles, The Making of a Christian Community in Late Antique Gaul,* Cambridge University Press, 1994

R. Latouche, *Caesar to Charlemagne: the beginnings of France,* trans. J. Nicholson, Barnes & Noble, 1968

A. W. Lawrence, *Greek Arms and Fortifications,* Oxford, 1979

J. Leach, *Pompey the Great,* Croom Helm, 1978

J. Lendering, *Gaius Julius Caesar,* Part Six, Civil Wars (51–47), ['Livius.Org'] <www.livius.org/caa-can/caesar/06.html>, viewed on 26 September 2010

J. Leversidge, *Everyday Life in the Roman Empire,* Batsford, 1976

A. M. Liberati and F. Bourbon, *Splendours of the Roman World,* Thames & Hudson, 1996

F. P. Long, *Caesar's Civil War with Pompeius,* Bk. II. 7, trans. F. P. Long, Oxford, 1906

Lucan, *Civil War,* Bk. 3, 310–314, trans. Susan. H. Braund, Oxford World's Classics, 1999

P. MacKendrick, *Roman France,* G. Bell & Sons, 1971

J-P. Morel, 'Phocaean Colonisation' in G. R. Tsetskhladze (ed.), *Greek Colonisation: An Account of Greek Colonies and Other Settlements Overseas,* vol.1, (Leiden, 2006): 358–428

E. W. Marsden, *Greek and Roman Artillery: Historical Development,* Oxford, 1969

S. P. Morris, 'Greeks and Barbarians–Linking with a wider world', in S. Alcock, and R. Osborne, (eds.), *Classical Archaeology*, Blackwell, 2007

Pliny the Elder, *Natural Histories*, vol.2, III, 34, trans. H. Rackham, Heinemann, 1947

E. Rawson, *Cicero: a portrait*, Allen Lane, 1975

A. L. F. Rivet, *Gallia Narbonensis,* Batsford, 1988

P. Rouillard., 'Greeks in the Iberian Peninsula', in M. Dietler and C. Lopez-Ruiz (eds.), *Colonial Encounters in Ancient Iberia: Phoenicians, Greeks and Indigenous Relations,* (University of Chicago Press, 2009)

I. D. Rowland, *Vitruvius Ten Books on Architecture*, Cambridge, 1999

R. Seagar, *Pompey: A Political Biography*, University of California Press, 1979

G. Shipley, *Pseudo-Skylax: The Circumnavigation of the Inhabited World-Text, Translation and Commentary*, 2-4, Bristol Phoenix Press, 2011

Strabo Geography, Vol. 2, IV.1.5, trans. H. L. Jones, Loeb, 1923

Suetonius, *Lives of the Twelve Caesars,* Julius Caesar, 24, Wordsworth Editions Ltd., 1999

Tacitus*, Agricola,* IV, trans. M. Hutton, Heinemann, 1980

B. Tang, *Delos, Carthage, Ampurias: the housing of three Mediterranean trading centres,* L'Erma di Bretschneider Rome, 2005

The Coinage of Julius Caesar, *Catalogue*, ['Macquarie University'] <www.humanities.mq.edu.au?acans/Caesar/Catalogue.htm>, viewed on 29 August 2011

The Elder Seneca, *Controversiae,* vol.1. 2.6.12, trans. M. Winterbottom, William Heinemann Ltd., 1974

The Numismatics of Celtic Warriors, (HCRI 19), D. R. Sear, *The History of Coinage of the Roman Imperators 49–27 B.C.* Spink, London, 1998, ISBN 090 0760 5982. <http://www.kernunnos.com/culture/warriors/>

The Roman History of Ammianus Marcellinus, XV.9. vol. 1. Loeb, 1935

J. Ussher, *The Annals of the World,* Master Books, 2003

Vitruvius: The Ten Books on Architecture, Bk. X. Ch. VI. 11, trans. M. H. Morgan, Dover Publication, 1960

H. White, *Appian's Roman History*, vol. 3. Bk. II. 41, Heinemann, 1913

G. Woolf, *Becoming Roman: the origins of provincial civilization in Gaul,* Cambridge University Press, 1998

SUGGESTED QUESTIONS AND TOPICS FOR DISCUSSION

Without Massalia's military, naval and financial help at crucial times would Rome have survived to become a world power?

Why was there Senatorial opposition to establishing the first Roman colony and port outside of Italy 118 B.C. at Narbo in Gaul? What were the arguments for and against?

Discuss the impact of the Greek city-state of Massalia (Marseille) on Gaul (France) and Iberia (Spain).

Discuss the strategic importance of Massalia (Marseille) in the Roman civil war between Pompey the Great and Julius Caesar and what measures were taken by both of them?

How did the Greek city-state of Massalia (Marseille) lose its empire? What stopped them from getting back their 'rights' and territories?

Discuss coin production in the Greek city-state of Massalia (Marseille) and what were its effects?

Cicero praises Massilia (Massalia) 'surrounded at the edge of the world by Gallic tribes'. Discuss the images he and others record of Massilia.

Discuss Phocaean and Massalia's colonies/settlements in the Western Mediterranean and why were they established?

How did the Celts, Helvetii and Druids know and write in Greek letters?

How did the Gallo-Greek and Iberian-Greek scripts come into use?

What ancient routes were available from the Mediterranean to get tin from Britain? What sources are there to prove this?

What route(s) did Pytheas of Marseille take in his discovery of Britain?

For the story of Marseille see C. Gunstone, *The Greek Empire of Marseille: Discoverer of Britain, Saviour of Rome*, Silver Shields, 2013.

INDEX

Agroitas
  Massalia school, 61
Albici
  ally of Massalia, 5, 18, 22
Apollo
  British coins, 2
Apollonides, 24
  commander of Massalia, 24, 54
  inscription, 59
Arles, 60, 63
  Siege of Massalia, 16, 17
  Sixth Legion, 43, 54
Artemis
  Caesar's victory coins, 46
Athenopolis, 43, 60
Battle of Frioul, 18
Battle of Tauroention, 21, 25, 28, 42
Brutus
  Massalia, 16, 17, 40, 43
Cicero
  civil war, 51
  Massalia, 53
  Massilia, 5, 52
Clodius, 47, 48
coins
  Britain, 2

Cornutus Scholiast to Lucan
  Massalia's commanders, 24, 25
Decimus Brutus, 16, 17, 54
  Battle of Frioul, 18
  Battle of Tauroention, 21
Emporion, 57
Galatae
  Massalia schools, 63
Gracchi
  Tiberius, 50
Hermon
  admiral of Massalia, 24, 25
inscriptions
  Massalia, 61
Julius Caesar
  Dictator, 41
  Greek script, 63
  Massalia, 5, 38
  Massalia victory coin, 46
  Milo, 48
L. Domitius Ahenobarbus
  Governer of Gaul, 9
Le Brusc, 21, 25, 28
Ligurians
  Hercules, 63
Lucan, 7, 9, 14, 18, 28, 33
  Massalia, 7, 14, 37
Marcus Brutus, 51, 55, 56
Marius, 17

Mark Antony, 53, 54, 55, 56, 60
  Massalia, 52, 57
Massalia
  Apollonides, 59
  commanders, 24
  fleet, 26
  independent city, 43
  necropolis, 59
  siege by Julius Caesar, 5
Milo, 47, 48
Moschus the Apollodorean
  Massalia school, 62
Nasidius
  admiral, 20, 21, 22, 25, 28, 54, 55
Octavian, 52, 56
Plutarch, 47
sacred grove, 44
Saguntum
  Lucan, 14
Sextus
  Apollonides, 54
  Cicero, 51
  Massalia, 56
  Massalia coins, 54
  Massilia, 53
Stoechades Islands, 43, 60
Tacitus, 62
Theline, 43

Thessaloniki
  Pompey the Great, 41
Trebonius
  Julius Caesar, 43
  killed, 52
  Massalia, 16, 33, 39, 40
Vitruvius
  Siege of Massalia, 34

NOTES

[1] A. Hermary, A. Hesnard, and H. Tréziny, *Marseille Grecque: La cite phocéenne (600–49 av. J-C)*, Editions Errance, 1999, p. 9 and p. 12.

[2] Strabo, *Geography*, V.2.2.

[3] T. J. Cornell, *The Beginning of Rome: Italy and Rome from the Bronze Age to the Punic Wars (c. 1000–264 B.C.)*, Routledge, 1995, p. 122.

[4] *Ibid*, p. 120.

[5] R. Latouche, *Caesar to Charlemagne: the beginnings of France*, trans. J. Nicholson, Barnes & Noble, 1968, p. 93; Ammianus Marcellinus, XV.11.

[6] B. Cunliffe, *The Extraordinary Voyage of Pytheas the Greek: The man who discovered Britain*, Penguin Books, 2002, p. 23.

[7] *The Roman History of Ammianus Marcellinus*, XV.9. vol. 1. Loeb, 1935, p. 177, ['Penelope. University of Chicago', digital library] <http://penelope.uchicago.edu/Thayer/E/Roman/Texts/Ammian/15*.html >, viewed 20 February 2012. (XV.9, p. 177 n. 62. Ammianus Marcellinus used as his source Timagenes of Alexandria who wrote *The History of the Gauls* in the first century B.C).

[8] P. de Jersey, *Celtic Coinage in Britain*, Shire, 2001, p. 20-21; Prototype coins L. de La Saussaye, *Numismatique de la Gaule Narbonnaise*, BLOIS Bureau de la Revue Numsimatique, 1842. Pl.VII No 368 & 369, p. 219; M. Feugère and M. Py, *Dictionnaire des monnaies découvertes en Gaule méditerranéenne* (530-27 avant notre ère), Éditions Monique Mergoil, 2011, p. 116, small bronze PBM-28 issue -275/-225 B.C., p. 114 MBM-34 issue -200/-150 B.C.

[9] P. Northover's email to me 13 March 2014; R. D. Van Arsdell, 'Earliest British Coinages' [Celtic Coinage of Britain] <http://vanarsdellcelticcoinageofbritain.com/history/earliest_british_coinages_1.html> viewed 31.12.2013.

[10] Diodorus Siculus, *Histories*, V.22, *The Library of History of Diodorus Siculus*, vol. 3. Loeb, 1939. ['Penelope, University of Chicago' digital library] <http://penelope.uchicago.edu/Thayer/E/Roman/Texts/Diodorus_Siculus/5B*.html#ref19> viewed 30 March 2012.

[11] G. Shipley, *Pseudo-Skylax: The Circumnavigation of the Inhabited World-Text, Translation and Commentary*, 2-4, Bristol Phoenix Press, 2011, p. 17 : B. Cunliffe, *The Extraordinary Voyage of Pytheas the Greek: The man who discovered Britain,* Penguin Books, 2002, p. 76.

[12] A. L. F. Rivet, *Gallia Narbonensis*, Batsford, 1988, p.

[13] Diodorus Siculus, *Histories*, V.22, *The Library of History of Diodorus Siculus,* vol. 3. Loeb, 1939. ['Penelope, University of Chicago' digital library] <http://penelope.uchicago.edu/Thayer/E/Roman/Texts/Diodorus_Siculus/5B*.html#ref19> viewed 30 March 2012.

[14] P. Attema, 'Conflict or Coexistence? Remarks on Indigenous Settlement and Colonization in the Foothills and Hinterland of the Sibaritde (Northern Calabria, Italy)' in P. G. Bilde and J. H. Petersen (eds.), *Meeting of Cultures in the Black Sea Region,* (University of Aarhus, 2008) :67-99, here p. 68-69 <http://www.pontos.dk/publications/books/bss-8-files/bss-8-04-attema>, viewed 12 February 2012. There were over 27 ancient Greek cities around the Black Sea coast, wealthy and on the tour circuit of actors from Athens and the latest plays.

[15] Cicero*, The Speeches: In Catilinam I–IV. Pro Murena. Pro Sulla. Pro Flacco*, trans. C. MacDonald, Heinemann, 1977, p. 511. *Pro Flacco* 63–64.

[16] Cicero, *De Officiis,* Bk. II. 8. 28–29, trans. W. Miller, Loeb, 1975, p.197. Banners illustrating victories were carried in processions.

[17] *Caesar's Civil War*, Chp. Bk. 1, Chp. XXXIV, trans. W.M. M'Devitte, G. Bell & Sons, 1928, p. 265.

[18] *Ibid,* Bk. 1, Chp. XXXV, p. 265.

[19] Caesar *The Civil War,* Bk. I.35, trans. J. Carter, Oxford's World Classics, 1998, p. 23.

[20] *Dio's Roman History*, vol.4. Bk. XLI, trans. E. Carey, Heinemann, 1916, p. 37.

[21] Lucan, *Civil War*, Bk. 3, 310–314, trans. Susan. H. Braund, Oxford World's Classics, 1999, p. 50.

[22] R. J. Rowland, Jnr., 'The Significance of Massilia in Lucan', *Hermes*, vol. 97, no. 2 (1969): 204–208, here p. 205, ['JSTOR' journal archive] <http://www.jstor.org/stable/4475586> viewed on 17 November 2009.

[23] J. Leach, *Pompey the Great*, Croom Helm, 1978, p. 184.

[24] Caesar, *The Civil War*, Bk. I.7, trans. J. Carter, Oxford's World Classics, 1998, p. 7.

[25] E. Rawson, *Cicero: a portrait*, Allen Lane, 1975, p. 137.

[26] Dr W. Smith, *A Smaller History of Rome*, John Murray, 1884, p. 232 – 234; T. Griffith, *Suetonius, Lives of the Twelve Caesars,* Julius Caesar, 24, Wordsworth Editions Ltd., 1999, p. 18.

[27] T. Griffith, *Suetonius, Lives of the Twelve Caesars*, Julius Caesar, 24, Wordsworth Editions Ltd., 1999, p. 18, and Nero, 2, p. 242.

[28] J. Lendering, *Gaius Julius Caesar*, Part Six, Civil Wars (51–47), ['Livius.Org'] <www.livius.org/caa-can/caesar/06.html>, viewed on 26 September 2010.

[29] T. Griffith, *Suetonius, Lives of the Twelve Caesars*, Julius Caesar, 34, Wordsworth Editions Ltd., 1999, p. 24; Domitius wants death but Caesar uses a pardon as a policy so that 'Magnus, all the Senate is–to be forgiven'. Domitius could not bear to owe anything to Caesar? Lucan, *Civil War*, II, 510-520. trans. S. H. Braund, Oxford, 1992, p. 35.

[30] Caesar, *The Civil War*, Bk. I, 34. trans. J. Carter, Oxford's World Classics, 1998, p. 22.

[31] J. Leach, *Pompey the Great*, Croom Helm, 1978, p. 184.

[32] Caesar, *The Civil War*, Bk. I. 34. trans. J. Carter, Oxford's World Classics, 1998, p. 22.

[33] *Ibid; The Works of Julius Caesar,* trans. W. S. McDevitte and W. S. Bohn,1869, <http://www.sacred-texts.com/cla/jcsr/civ1.htm> viewed 22 April 2013.

[34] Caesar, *The Civil War,* Bk. I. 35. trans. J. Carter, Oxford's World Classics, 1998, p. 23.

[35] *Ibid,* Bk. I. 36, p. 23.

[36] T. Griffith, *Suetonius, Lives of the Twelve Caesars,* Nero, 2, Wordsworth Editions Ltd., 1999, p. 242.

[37] *Lucan: Civil War,* Bk. III. 388–393, trans. Susan H. Braund, Oxford World's Classics, 1999, p. 53.

[38] *Ibid*, Bk. III. 307–309, p. 50.

[39] *Ibid,* Bk. III. 349–350, p. 51. In Book III. 298–762 Lucan describes the siege and in graphic detail one of the two naval battles of Massalia allied to Pompey, which ended in defeat by Caesar's ships. Strabo (III.4.6) mentions that Saguntum was a Massaliote city though by origin founded by Zakynthos.

[40] Caesar had ten legions. The sixteenth legion crossed the Rubicon with him in Italy leaving nine legions in Gaul numbered between one and fifteen. Legions 1 to 4 and 9 are not accounted for in the list given on the Livius.com website and the three legions Caesar had at Massalia may have been from these? J. Lendering, *Gaius Julius Caesar,* Part six, ['Livius.com'] <www.livius.org/caa-can/caesar/06.html> viewed on 26 September 2010.

[41] Caesar, *The Civil War,* Bk. I. 36, trans. J. Carter, Oxford's World Classics, 1998, p. 279 n. 1.36.

[42] *Dio's Roman History*, vol.4, Book XLI.19, trans. E. Cary, Loeb Classical Library, William Heinemann, 1916, p. 37.

[43] *Caesar's Civil War,* Bk. I, Chp. XXXV, trans. W. A. M'Devitte, G. Bell & Sons, 1928, p. 265.

[44] R. Gardiner, (ed.), *The Age of the Galley,* Conway Maritime Press, 1995, p.70.

[45] Caesar, *The Civil War,* Bk. I, 36. trans. J. Carter, Oxford's World Classics, 1998, p. 23.

[46] *Ibid,* Bk. I, 39 & 41, p. 24–5.

[47] I. D. Rowland, *Vitruvius Ten Books on Architecture*, Cambridge, 1999, p. 317, Commentary: Book 10, Massilia (10.16.11–12) (Figure 139).

[48] Strabo, *Geography,* IV.1.5.

[49] W. W. Bateson and C. Damon, *Caesar's Civil War,* Oxford, 2006, p. 127. (Caesar, *B.C.* 2.4.4).

[50] Michele Clerc Directeur du Musée archéologique de Marseille (1895-1928)

[51] M. Clerc, *Massalia: Histoire de Marseille dans L'Antiquité des Origins a la Fin de l'empire Romain d'occident*, vol. 2, Librarie A. Tacussel, 1929, p. 117.

[52] P. MacKendrick, *Roman France,* G. Bell & Sons, 1971, p. 11.

[53] Lucan, *Civil War*, Bk. III. 560–566, trans. Susan. H. Braund, Oxford World's Classics, 1999, p. 56.

[54] *Caesar's Civil War*, Bk. 1, Chp. LVIII, trans. W. A. M'Devitte, G. Bell & Sons, 1928, p. 275.

[55] Lucan, *Civil War*, Bk. III. 298-762, trans. Susan. H. Braund, Oxford World's Classics, 1999.

[56] Suetonius, *The Lives of the Caesars*, The Deified Julius, vol. 1. LXVIII.4, trans. J. C. Rolfe, Heinemann, 1979, p. 91.

[57] Caesar, *The Civil War,* Bk. II.3–4, trans. J. Carter, Oxford, 1998, p. 51.

[58] *Ibid*, p. 51.

[59] Caesar, *The Civil War*, Bk. II. 4, trans. J. Carter, Oxford, 1998, p. 51.

[60] *Ibid*, p. 51–52.

[61] *Ibid*, p. 51.

[62] *Caesar's Civil War with Pompeius,* Bk. II.5–7, trans. F. P. Long, Oxford, 1906, p. 95.

[63] Caesar, *The Civil War,* Bk. II.5, trans. J. Carter, Oxford, 1998, p. 53.

[64] *Ibid*, p. 52.

[65] Caesar's *Civil War with Pompeius*, Bk. II. 5, trans. F. P. Long, Oxford, 1906, p. 76.

[66] Caesar, *The Civil War*, Bk. II.7, trans. J. Carter, Oxford, 1998, p. 53.

[67] *Caesar's Civil War with Pompeius,* Bk. II.5–7, trans F. P. Long, Oxford, 1906, p. 76–78.

[68] Caesar, *The Civil War*, Bk. II. 7, trans. J. Carter, Oxford, 1998, p. 53.

[69] F. P. Long, *Caesar's Civil War with Pompeius,* Bk. II. 7, trans. F. P. Long, Oxford, 1906, p. 78.

[70] M. Clerc, *Massalia: Histoire de Marseille dans L'Antiquité des Origins a la Fin de l'empire Romain d'occident*, vol. 2, Librarie A. Tacussel, 1929, p. 179.

[71] <https://www.ancient-origins.net/sites/default/files/styles/large/public/Naval.jpg?itok=kukuAGSx> viewed 12.01.2022.

[72] A. M. Liberati and F. Bourbon, *Splendours of the Roman World*, Thames & Hudson, 1996, p. 218.

[73] A. Trevor. Hodge, *Ancient Greek France,* University of Pennsylvania, 1999, p. 104.

[74] *Ibid*, p. 104 n. 34; M. Clerc, *Massalia*, 2 vols. (Marseille, 1927–9; reprint Lafitte, Marseille, 1971) 2, p. 78 n. 2 & 2, p. 123 n. 1.

[75] A. Trevor. Hodge, *Ancient Greek France*, University of Pennsylvania, 1999, p. 103–104, p. 255 n. 34 and n. 36. Lucius Anneas Cornutus from Leptis and in Rome during the reign of Emperor Nero. M. Fröhner, 'Scolies latines relative a l'histoire et a la topographie de Marseille', *Revue Archéologique*, XVIII, II, (1891): 321-332, here p. 325.

Lucan's epic poem *Pharsalia* (*Di Bello Civili,* The Civil War) was written in ten books (all survive and the tenth was unfinished). The later books became more pro-republican and anti-imperial. Nero and Lucan, at first friends had a falling out and Lucan was forbidden to publish his poems. Lucan continued writing insulting poem about Nero, which he ignored. Unfortunately for Lucan he joined the Piso conspiracy A.D. 65 and on being discovered Nero forced Lucan to commit suicide at the age of 25.
[76] *Ibid*, p. 106.

[77] M. Fröhner, 'Scolies latines relative a l'histoire et a la topographie de Marseille', *Revue Archéologique*, XVIII, II, (1891): 321-332, here p. 325-326, Scholiast to Lucan III.524.

[78] M. Clerc, *Massalia: Histoire de Marseille dans L'Antiquité des Origins a la Fin de l'empire Romain d'occident*, vol. 2. 1929, p. 78, & n. 2.

[79] *Strabo Geography,* Vol. 2, IV.1.5, trans. H. L. Jones, Loeb, 1923, p. 175 n. 3.
[80] *Ibid*.

[81] M. Clerc, *Massalia: Histoire de Marseille dans L'Antiquité des Origins a la Fin de l'empire Romain d'occident*, vol. 2, Librarie A. Tacussel, 1929, p. 78 n. 2; (*Revue Archéologique*, 1891, XVIII, II, p. 322). Praetor is translated for stratigos, army leader, general.
[82] *Ibid*, p. 123 n. 1, (*Revue Archéologique*, 1891, XVIII, II, p. 325-326), Scholiast to Lucan III.524. Fröhner gives the reference M. H. Usener, *Scholia in Lucani bellum civile; commenta Bernensia*, 1869, (Leipzig, chez Teubneri) which is now available to download online at <http://archive.org/details/scholiainlucani00usengoog>, viewed 5 June 2012.

[83] D. Mercer, *Chronicle of the Twentieth Century*, 21 April 1932, Longman, 1998, p. 392.

[84] *Ibid*, p. 450.

[85] Strabo, *Geography,* IV. 1.5.28.

[86] *Ibid*.

[87] *Ibid.*

[88] A. Trevor. Hodge, *Ancient Greek France*, University of Pennsylvania, 1999, p. 103 n. 33. Caes. *B.C.* 1. 34–6, 56–8; 2,1–16. Lucan, *Pharsalia*, 3, 30–374, Vell.Pat. 2 50. Dio Cass. 41.19. Rivet, 65–66.

[89] A. Trevor. Hodge, *Ancient Greek France*, University of Pennsylvania, 1999, p. 255 n. 37; M. Clerc, *Massalia: Histoire de Marseille dans L'Antiquité des Origins a la Fin de l'empire Romain d'occident*, vol. 2. Librarie A. Tacussel, 1929, p. 127. n. 1, Plutarch, Pompey, 64.

[90] H. White, *Appian's Roman History*, vol. 3. Bk. II. 41, Heinemann, 1913, p. 305. Julius Caesar appointed Hortensius and Dollabella admirals while both fleets were under construction.

[91] A. Trevor. Hodge, *Ancient Greek France*, University of Pennsylvania, 1999, p. 103.

[92] H. White, *Appian's Roman History,* vol. 3. Bk. II, ch. 11, Heinemann, 1913, p. 379.

[93] T. Griffith, *Suetonius, Lives of the Twelve Caesars,* Nero, 2, Wordsworth Editions Ltd., 1999, p. 242.

[94] H. White, *Appian's Roman History*, vol. 3. Bk. I, ch. 10, Heinemann, 1913, p. 359.

[95] J. Leach, *Pompey the Great,* Croom Helm, 1978, p. 188.

[96] M. Clerc, *Massalia: Histoire de Marseille dans L'Antiquité des Origins a la Fin de l'empire Romain d'occident*, vol. 2, Librarie A. Tacussel, 1929, p.78 n.2;(RA, 1891, XVIII, II, p. 322).

[97] Lucan, *The Civil War*, Book 3, 575–580, trans. N. Rowe, Everyman, 1998, p. 75.

[98] Caesar, *The Civil War*, Bk. I.36, trans. J. Carter, Oxford, 1998, p. 23.

[99] R. Seagar, *Pompey: A Political Biography*, University of California Press, 1979, p. 178.

[100] T. Griffith, *Suetonius, Lives of the Twelve Caesars*, Julius Caesar, 34, Wordsworth Editions Ltd., 1999, p. 24.

[101] Caesar, *The Civil War*, Bk. II.17–18, trans. J. Carter, Oxford, 1998, p. 59.

[102] *Ibid*, p. 61.

[103] M. Clerc, *Massalia: Histoire de Marseille dans L'Antiquité des Origins a la Fin de l'empire Romain d'occident*, vol. 2, Librarie A. Tacussel, 1929, p. 209.

[104] A. W. Lawrence, *Greek Arms and Fortifications,* Oxford, 1979, p. 93–95.

[105] Caesar, *The Civil War*, Bk. II.1, trans. J. Carter, Oxford, 1998, p. 50.

[106] Caesar, *The Civil War,* Bk. 2.2.2, trans. J. Carter, Oxford, 1998, p. 50.

[107] A. W. Lawrence, *Greek Arms and Fortifications,* Oxford, 1979, p. 95, Caesar, *B.C.* 2.2.2.

[108] A. W. Lawrence, *Greek Arms and Fortifications,* Oxford, 1979, p. 95, (Lucan, III.685–695): for a diagram showing effective cross-fire ranges of catapults from the city wall towers see Lawrence p. 155, Diagram 1.

[109] A. Hermary, A. Hesnard, and H. Tréziny, *Marseille Grecque: La cite phocéenne (600–49 av. J-C),* Editions Errance, 1999, p. 152.

[110] A. W. Lawrence, *Greek Arms and Fortifications,* Oxford, 1979, p. 93–95; 'Roman lead sling bullets found at the siege of Perusia 41/40 B.C. were marked with thunderbolt motifs, some with names of centurions and legions, others with obscene insults of its intended target such as the intimate parts of Mark Antony's wife Fulvia'. D. B. Campbell, *Siege Warfare in the Roman World* 146 BC–AD 378, Osprey Publishing, 2005, p. 29.

[111] Caesar, *The Civil War*, Bk. II. 1, trans. J. Carter, Oxford, 1998, p. 50.

[112] A. Hermary, A. Hesnard, and H. Tréziny, *Marseille Grecque: La cite phocéenne (600–49 av. J-C),* Editions Errance, 1999, p. 152.

[113] Caesar, *The Civil War*, Bk. II.1, trans. J. Carter, Oxford, 1998, p. 50.
[114] *Ibid*, Bk. II.11, p. 55–56.

[115] *Vitruvius: The Ten Books on Architecture,* Bk. X. Ch. VI. 11, trans. M. H. Morgan, Dover Publication, 1960, p. 318.

[116] *Ibid*, Bk. X, Ch. VI. 12, p. 318.

[117] E. W. Marsden, *Greek and Roman Artillery: Historical Development,* Oxford, 1969, p. 113 n. 2, Caesar, *Civil War*, 16.3.

[118] Caesar, *The Civil War*, Bk. II.16. trans J. Carter, Oxford, 1998, p. 58.

[119] Lucan, *Civil War*, Bk. 3. 463–480, trans. Susan. H. Braund, Oxford World's Classics, 1999, p. 54.

[120] Caesar, *The Civil War*, Bk. II.11. trans J. Carter, Oxford, 1998, p. 56.

[121] W. W. Bateson and C. Damon, *Caesar's Civil War*, 2.12. 3–4, Oxford, 2006, p. 159.

[122] Caesar, *The Civil War*, Bk. II.13. trans J. Carter, Oxford, 1998, p. 56.

[123] *Ibid.*

[124] *Ibid*, Bk. II.14, p. 57.

[125] *Dio's Roman History*, vol.6, Bk. XLI, trans. E. Carey, Heinemann, 1916, p. 47.

[126] Caesar, *The Civil War*, Bk. II.13. trans J. Carter, Oxford, 1998, p. 57.

[127] *Ibid.* Bk. II.13. p. 57.

[128] *Ibid*, Bk. II.15. p. 57.

[129] *Ibid*, Bk. II.15. p. 58.

[130] *Ibid.*

[131] *Ibid*, Bk.II. 22, p. 62.

[132] *Ibid.*

[133] *Ibid*, Bk. II. 16, p. 58.
[134] *Ibid*.
[135] *Ibid*, Bk. II. 18, p. 59.
[136] *Ibid*, Bk. II. 22, p. 62.

[137] F. P. Long, *Caesar's Civil War with Pompeius*, Bk. II. 14, trans. F. P. Long, Oxford, 1906, p. 76.

[138] Caesar, *The Civil War*, Bk.II, 22 trans J. Carter, Oxford's World Classics, 1998, p. 62.

[139] T. Griffith, *Suetonius, Lives of the Twelve Caesars*, Nero, 2, Wordsworth Editions Ltd., 1999, p. 242.

[140] Caesar, *The Civil War*, Bk. II. 22, trans. J. Carter, Oxford's World Classics, 1998, p. 62–63.

[141] *Dio's Roman History*, vol. 4, Book XLI.19, trans. E. Cary, William Heinemann, Loeb Classical Library, 1916, p. 47.

[142] M. Clerc, *Massalia: Histoire de Marseille dans L'Antiquité des Origins a la Fin de l'empire Romain d'occident*, vol. 2, Librarie A. Tacussel, 1927, p. 127 n. 4, Lucan V.53, cf Dion, XLI, 25.

[143] Caesar, *The Civil War*, Bk. II. 22, trans. J. Carter, Oxford's World Classics, 1998, p. 63.

[144] *Ibid*, p. 62.

[145] R. Seagar, *Pompey: A Political Biography*, University of California Press, 1979, p. 178.

[146] Appian, *The Civil Wars*, Book II. 48, trans. J. Carter, Penguin, 1996, p. 372 n. 103.

[147] *Ibid*, Book II, 47, p. 93–94.

[148] *Ibid*, Book II. 48, p. 94.

[149] *Ibid*, Book II. 48, p. 372 n. 101.

[150] Cicero, *Letters to Atticus*, vol. 3. 183 (IX.15), trans. D. R. Shackleton Bailey, Harvard University Press, 1999, p. 87.

[151] Caesar, *The Civil War*, Bk. I.35–36, trans. J. Carter, Oxford's World Classics, 1998, 23.

[152] *Ibid*, Bk. II. 14, p. 57.

[153] *Dio's Roman History*, vol.6. Bk. XLI, trans. E. Carey, Heinemann, 1916, p. 37.

[154] W. W. Bateson and C. Damon, Caesars' Civil War, Oxford, 2006, p. 128, Caesar, *B.C.* II.22.

[155] M. Clerc, *Massalia: Histoire de Marseille dans L'Antiquité des Origins a la Fin de l'empire Romain d'occident*, vol. 2, Librarie A. Tacussel, 1927, p. 155.

[156] A. Trevor. Hodge, *Ancient Greek France*, University of Pennsylvania Press, 1999, p. 175–176.

[157] P. MacKendrick, *Roman France*, G. Bell & Sons, 1971, p. 11.

[158] Caesar, *The Civil War*, Bk. I. 36, trans. J Carter, Oxford's World Classics, 1998, p. 23.

[159] H. Cleere, *Southern France: An Oxford Archaeological Guide*, Oxford, 2001, p. 111, Caesar, *Civil War* 1.36.

[160] G. Magi, *Provence*, Casa Editrice Bonechi, 2001, p. 81.

[161] H. Cleere, *Southern France: An Oxford Archaeological Guide*, Oxford, 2001, p.138.

[162] A. Hermary, A. Hesnard, A., and H. Tréziny, *Marseille Grecque: La cite phocéenne (600–49 av. J-C)*, Editions Errance, 1999, p. 155 n. 35 Tacitus, *Histories*, 3.43; M. Bats, 'The Greeks in Gaul and Corsica: the rhythm of the Greek emporion' in P. Carratelli (ed.), *The Western Greeks: Classical Civilization in the Western Mediterranean*, (London, 1996): 577–584, here p. 581; Pliny, *NH*, III.5.

[163] *Appian's Roman History,* vol. 3. Bk. II. 48, trans. H. White, Heinemann, 1913, p. 317.

[164] Trebonius published a collection of his friend Cicero's witty sayings and puns in 47 B.C. He became *pro-praetor* of Spain 47-46 B.C. Caesar rewarded his loyalty with a Consulship 45 B.C. and promise of being the Governor of Asia. Trebonius then joined the conspiracy to murder Caesar in 44 B.C. and detained Mark Antony at the door of the Senate on the day. Trebonius left Rome to become Governor of Asia and was murdered in Smyrna 43 B.C. on the orders of Dollabella becoming the first of Caesar's murderers to die. M. Bunson, *A Dictionary of the Roman Empire*, Oxford, 1990, p. 426; 'Appian, The Civil Wars', III.26, *The Histories of Appian,* Loeb, 1913, p. 567, ['Penelope' University of Chicago digital library] <http://penelope.uchicago.edu/Thayer/E/Roman/Texts/Appian/Civil_Wars/3*.html> viewed 14 May 2012, Cassius Dio, vol.5.46.49; Sacred grove outside Massalia, Lucan, *Civil War*, III.445, trans. S. H. Braund, Oxford, 1992, p. 53. See also A. Augoustakis, 'Cutting Down the Grove in Lucan, Valerius Maximus and Dio Cassius', *The Classical Quarterly*, vol. 56, No. 2 (Dec, 2006):634-638 <www.jstor.org/stable/4493456>.

[165] The Coinage of Julius Caesar, *Catalogue,* ['Macquarie University'] <www.humanities.mq.edu.au?acans/Caesar/Catalogue.htm>, viewed on 29 August 2011.

[166] *The Numismatics of Celtic Warriors*, (HCRI 19), D. R. Sear, *The History of Coinage of the Roman Imperators 49–27 B.C.* Spink, London, 1998, ISBN 090 0760 5982. <http://www.kernunnos.com/culture/warriors/>, viewed on 29 August 2011.

[167] J. Leversidge, *Everyday Life in the Roman Empire*, Batsford, 1976, p. 90.

[168] Cicero, *Pro Milone*, Appendix, trans. N. H. Watts, Heinemann, 1931, appendix from the Commentary of Quintus Asconius Pedianus, p. 124.
[169] *Ibid*, p. 134, note a.
[170] *Ibid*, Appendix, p. 136.

[171] G. P. Kelly, *A History of Exile in the Roman Republic,* Cambridge, 2006, p. 134.

[172] *Ibid*, p. 126.

[173] Cicero, *Pro Milone*, trans. N. H. Watts, Heinemann, 1972, p. 5; Dr W. Smith, *A Smaller History of Rome*, John Murray, 1884, p. 238.

[174] *Dio's Roman History*, vol. 3. XL, trans. E. Carey, Heinemann, 1914, p. 489.

[175] H. White, *Appian's Roman History*, vol. 3. II. 48, Heinemann, 1913, p. 317; J. Carter, *Appian The Civil Wars*, Book II, 48, Penguin, 1996, p. 94.

[176] Cicero, *Pro Milone*, Appendix from the Commentary of Quintus Asconius Podianus, trans. N. H. Watts, Heinemann, 1931, p. 135.

[177] *Justin: Epitome of the Philippic History of Pompeius Trogus*, 38.6.7, trans. J. C. Yardley, Scholars Press Atlanta, GA, 1994, p. 241.

[178] T. J. Cornell, *The Beginning of Rome: Italy and Rome from the Bronze Age to the Punic Wars (c. 1000–264 B.C.)*, Routledge, 1995, p. 148.

[179] *Ibid*, p. 150.
[180] *Ibid*, p. 148.
[181] *Ibid*, p. 150.

[182] *Cicero Letters to Atticus*, vol. 3, XIV. 13, trans. E. O. Winstedt, Heinemann, 1961, p. 243.

[183] *Ibid*, vol. 3, XIV. 14, p. 258–259; Possibly Massilians ambassadors were neighbours of Atticus in Rome. W. Guthrie, *Cicero's Epistles to Atticus: With Notes, Historical, Explanatory, and Critical*, vol. 3, London, 1806, p.225 n.1.

[184] P. Bayle, A. Tricaud, and A. Gaudin, *The Dictionary Historical and Critical of Mr. Peter Bayle*, vol. 2, London, 1735, p. 680.
<http://books.google.co.uk/books?id=QE8hAQAAMAAJ&pg=PA680&lpg=PA680&dq=Trebonius+killed+by+Dolabella+when?&source=bl&ots=Q3CLxtx4ir&sig=dv3B7gbm2ptW6i7GqOoJWBTaT-I&hl=en&sa=X&ei=8167T_auH8fD8QOt79nRCg&ved=0CFgQ6AEwBg#v=onepage&q=Trebonius%20killed%20by%20Dolabella%20when%3F&f=false>
viewed on 22 May 2012; *43 B.C. Olympiad 184.2*, ['Attalus']
<http://www.attalus.org/bc1/year43.html#7> viewed on 22 May 2012.

[185] J. Ussher, *The Annals of the World,* Master Books, 2003, p. 676; Cicero, *Philippics*: 3-9, Edited with Introduction, Translation and Commentary,Vol. 2, Commentary, by G. Manuwald, Walter de Gruyter, 2007, p. 906-7.

[186] *Cicero Philippic,* XIII. xv. 30–32, trans. W. Ker, Loeb, 1926, p. 583.

[187] *Ibid,* XIII. v. 12–vi, 14, p. 559.

[188] S. Dando-Collins, *Cleopatra's Kidnappers: How Caesar's Sixth Legion Gave Egypt to Rome and Rome to Caesar*, John Wiley & Sons, 2005, p. 222-241.

[189] *Appian's Roman History,* IV, 11, 84, trans. H. White, Heinemann, 1913, p. 281.

[190] *Appian's Roman History*, III, 4. trans. H. White, Heinemann, 1964, p. 523.

[191] *Ibid,* III, 4. p. 523.
[192] *Ibid*, III, 3. p. 521-523.

[193] *Ibid*, III, 4. p. 525. ['Penelope, University of Chicago' digital library] <http://penelope.uchicago.edu/Thayer/E/Roman/Texts/Appian/Civil_Wars/3*.html>, viewed 27 May 2012.

[194] M. Clerc, *Massalia: Histoire de Marseille dans L'Antiquité des Origins a la Fin de l'empire Romain d'occident*, vol. 2, Librarie A. Tacussel, 1929, p. 246 n.1.

[195] Appian The Civil Wars, II, 135, *The Histories of Appian*, Loeb, 1913, p. 477, ['Penelope, University of Chicago' digital library] <http://penelope.uchicago.edu/Thayer/E/Roman/Texts/Appian/Civil_Wars/2*.html >, viewed 7 February 2012.

[196] *Appian The Civil Wars*, III, 1. 2, ['Perseus, University of Chicago' digital library] <http://perseus.uchicago.edu/perseus-cgi/citequery3.pl?dbname=Greek Texts&query=App.%20BC%203.1&getid=1 >, viewed 7 February 2012.

[197] *Appian The Civil Wars,* IV, 11, 84, H. White (ed.),Macmillan & Co., 1899, ['Perseus' Tufts university digital library], <http://www.perseus.tufts.edu/hopper/text?doc=Perseus%3Atext%3A199 9.01.0232%3Abook%3D4%3Achapter%3D11%3Asection%3D84> viewed 21 May 2012.

[198] A. L. F. Rivet, *Gallia Narbonensis,* Batsford, 1988, p.75 n. 37.

[199] *Appian's Roman History,* IV, ch. XI, 84, trans. H. White, Heinemann, 1913, p. 299.

[200] *Ibid,* IV, ch. XII, 95, p. 281.
[201] *Ibid,* V, ch. VIII, 67, p. 491.
[202] *Ibid,* V, ch. VIII, 72, p. 500–511.
[203] *Ibid,* V, ch. XI, 100, p. 547.
[204] *Ibid,* V, ch. XIV, 140 & 144, p. 609–615.

[205] *Appian's Roman History,* V. ch. 1, 3, trans. H. White, Heinemann, 1913, p. 381.

[206] *Ibid,* Bk. V. ch. XIII, 126, p. 587.

[207] M. Clerc, *Massalia: Histoire de Marseille dans L'Antiquité des Origins a la Fin de l'empire Romain d'occident*, vol. 2. Librarie A. Tacussel, 1929, p. 246 n. 1.

The city of Thessaloniki had also supported Pompey and the losing side. Subsequently they took extraordinary steps to gain favour with Octavian Caesar (Augustus) by dismantling a large sixth-century temple of Aphrodite at Aeneia on the Thermaic gulf: re-erecting it in Thessaloniki: and dedicated to Octavian. Aeneia was said to have been founded by Aeneas from Troy, *(Ancient coins of Macedonia)*, <http://www.snible.org/coins/hn/macedon.html>, viewed on 28 August 2010), and Julius Caesar had claimed descent from Aphrodite. Part of the temple and statues can be seen in the Archaeological Museum Thessaloniki Greece.

[208] M. Clerc, *Massalia: Histoire de Marseille dans L'Antiquité des Origins a la Fin de l'empire Romain d'occident*, vol. 2. Librarie A. Tacussel, 1929, p. 247 n.1. Livy, XXXIV, 9.

[209] *Appian's Roman History,* Bk. V, ch. XIV, 137, trans. H. White, Heinemann, 1913, p. 605.

[210] B. Tang, *Delos, Carthage, Ampurias: the housing of three Mediterranean trading centres,* L'Erma di Bretschneider Rome, 2005, p.113

[211] P. Rouillard., 'Greeks in the Iberian Peninsula', in M. Dietler and C. Lopez-Ruiz (eds.), *Colonial Encounters in Ancient Iberia: Phoenicians, Greeks and Indigenous Relations,* (University of Chicago Press, 2009): 131-154, here p. 141.

[212] Strabo, *Geography,* III.4.8

[213] D. Baatz, 'Recent Finds of Ancient Artillery', *Brittania,* Vol. 9 (1978), pp. 1-17, Society for the Promotion of Roman Studies, ['JSTOR' journal archive] <https://www.jstor.org/stable/525936> viewed 25.01.2022

[214] H. Cleere, *Southern France: An Oxford Archaeological Guide,* Oxford, 2001, p. 138.

[215] *Ibid,* p. 125.

[216] M. Clerc, *Massalia: Histoire de Marseille dans L'Antiquité des Origins a la Fin de l'empire Romain d'occident,* Librarie A. Tacussel, vol. 2, 1929, p. 78. *IGIS,* vol. XIV, 2454; CF, n° 105; *IGF* 17, p. 28.

[217] *Ibid,* Clerc, 1929, p. 78.

[218] *Ibid,* p. 324, *IG* 2454, *Inscriptiones Graecia,* vol. XIV. Appendix, Inscriptiones Galliae, III, Massalia, 2454. Berolini, 1890, p. 647. See *IG,* XIV, 2454 for exact spacing of inscription letters; the Pye and Ita in Pompeius are joined together.

[219] G. H. R. Horsley, *New Documents Illustrating Early Christianity: A Review of the Greek Inscriptions and Papyrii published in 1979,* vol. 4, Macquarie University, 1987, p. 156.

[220] M. Clerc, *Massalia: Histoire de Marseille dans L'Antiquité des Origins a la Fin de l'empire Romain d'occident*, vol. 2. Librarie A. Tacussel, 1929, p. 247; M. Bats, 'The Greeks in Gaul and Corsica: the rhythm of the Greek emporion' in P. Carratelli (ed.), *The Western Greeks: Classical Civilization in the Western Mediterranean*, (London, 1996): 577–584, here p. 581; Pliny, *NH*, III.5.

[221] A. Trevor. Hodge, *Ancient Greek France*, University of Pennsylvania, 1999, p. 179–182. A few Massaliote coins have been found on the beach at Cannes.

[222] H. Cleere, *Southern France: An Oxford Archaeological Guide*, Oxford, 2001, p. 138.

[223] Pliny the Elder, *Natural Histories*, vol.2, III, 34, trans. H. Rackham, Heinemann, 1947, p. 29.

[224] Strabo, *Geography*, IV.1.5.

[225] W. E. Klingshirn, *Caesarius of Arles, The Making of a Christian Community in Late Antique Gaul*, Cambridge University Press, 1994, p. 37.

[226] Strabo, *Geography*, IV. 1.5.27-28.

[227] The Elder Seneca, *Controversiae*, vol.1. 2.6.12, trans. M. Winterbottom, William Heinemann Ltd., 1974, p. 361.

[228] *Ibid*, vol.1. 2.5.13, p. 333.

[229] Strabo, *Geography*, IV.1. 5.

[230230] Tacitus, *Agricola*, IV, trans. M. Hutton, Heinemann, 1980, p. 33.

[231] S. P. Morris, 'Greeks and Barbarians–Linking with a wider world', in S. Alcock, and R. Osborne, (eds.), *Classical Archaeology*, Blackwell, 2007, p. 391.

[232] *Justin: Epitome of the Philippic History of Pompeius Trogus,* 43.4.1, trans. J. C. Yardley, Scholars Press Atlanta, GA, 1994, 267.

[233] M. Bats, 'The Greeks in Gaul and Corsica: the rhythm of the Greek emporion', P. Carratelli (ed.), *The Western Greeks: classical civilization in the Western Mediterranean* (London, 1996): 577–584, here p. 583.

[234] Strabo, *Geography*, vol.2. IV. I. 5, trans. H. L. Jones. Loeb, 1969, p. 179.

[235] Caesar, *The Gallic War*, I.29, trans. H. J. Edwards, Dover, 2006, p. 14.
[236] *Ibid*, II.28. p. 41.
[237] *Ibid*, VI.14. p. 103.

[238] For comparison of Gallo-Greek and Greek-Iberian scripts see M. Dietler, 'The Iron Age in Mediterranean France: Colonial Encounters and Transformations'. *Journal of World Prehistory*, Vol. 11. No. 3. (1997): 269-358, here p. 305-307.

<http://chicago.academia.edu/MichaelDietler/Papers/218412/The_Iron_Age_In_Mediterranean_France_Colonial_Encounters_Entanglements_and_Transformations>, viewed 6 February 2012.

[239] G. Woolf, *Becoming Roman: the origins of provincial civilization in Gaul*, Cambridge University Press, 1998, p. 92.

[240] A. Trevor. Hodge, *Ancient Greek France*, University of Pennsylvania, 1999, p. 160.
[241] *Ibid*, p. 220.
[242] *Ibid*, p. 36.

[243] J-P. Morel, 'Phocaean Colonisation' in G. R. Tsetskhladze (ed.), *Greek Colonisation: An Account of Greek Colonies and Other Settlements Overseas*, vol.1, (Leiden, 2006): 358–428, here p. 380, (Aeschylus *apud*, Strabo 4.1.7).

[244] A. Trevor. Hodge, *Ancient Greek France*, University of Pennsylvania, 1999, p. 46.

[245] Pliny the Elder, *Natural Histories*, vol.2, III, 34, trans. H. Rackham, Heinemann, 1947, p. 29.

Printed in Great Britain
by Amazon